ALLEN COUNTY PUBLIC LIBRARY
FORT WAYNE, INDIANA 46802

You may return this book to any location of
the Allen County Public Library.

DEMCO

SUPERCOMPUTERS
V

FACTS ON FILE SCIENCE SOURCEBOOKS

SUPERCOMPUTERS
SHAPING THE FUTURE

CHARLENE W. BILLINGS

Facts On File®

AN INFOBASE HOLDINGS COMPANY

Supercomputers: Shaping the Future

Facts On File, Inc.
460 Park Avenue South
New York NY 10016

Library of Congress Cataloging-in-Publication Data

Billings, Charlene W.
    Supercomputers : shaping the future / Charlene W. Billings.
       p.   cm. — (Facts On File science sourcebooks)
    Includes bibliographical references and index.
    ISBN 0-8160-3096-0 (acid-free paper)
    1. Supercomputers—Juvenile literature. [1. Supercomputers. 2. Computers.]
  I. Title. II. Series
  QA76.88.B55 1995
  004.1′ 1—dc20
                                             94-44111

Text design by Catherine Rincon Hyman
Cover design by Amy Gonzalez
Illustrations by Marc Greene
On the cover: A researcher wearing a virtual reality headset and data glove.

Other Books by Charlene W. Billings

*T*o the computer pioneers

*E*xtraordinary change is possible when enough courageous people grasp the need for it and become willing to act.

—Sandra Postal,
Worldwatch Institute,
in *State of the World 1992*

CONTENTS

ACKNOWLEDGMENTS

*M*y sincere appreciation to everyone who has helped to provide information and photographs for this book. Special thanks to the staff members at the National Center for Supercomputing Applications and the San Diego Supercomputer Center for their assistance.

1

$\vee$

WHAT IS A SUPERCOMPUTER?

---

*S*upercomputers are the fastest, most powerful computers in the world. Scientists and business people use them to solve complex problems in research and industry. Because supercomputers can rapidly analyze enormous quantities of numerical data, they are sometimes called number crunchers.

Into the Age of Teraflops and Beyond

Supercomputers have now thrust us toward the age of teraflops—a time when they can complete over one trillion *flops*, or floating point operations, per second. Why do we need computers that are capable of higher and higher speeds of performance?

Supercomputers are used by scientific researchers to study complex problems such as weather forecasting and earthquakes, by industries to design products such as high-performance aircraft and computer chips, and by businesses to create realistic virtual reality environments for practical applications as well as for entertainment.

1

A four-processor CRAY Extended Architecture computer system from Cray Research, Inc., Minneapolis. (Courtesy Cray Research, Inc.)

One of the most pressing reasons we need supercomputers is that the world's store of information is doubling approximately every five years. For information to be useful, it must be processed, accessible, and applied. An example is the data that is being sent back to Earth from the Hubble telescope and from research satellites in space. Even with access to powerful, high-speed computers, it will take years for researchers to analyze all of the information being received from these space-based sources alone.

Many of the problems being studied by scientists are too complex for even the fastest computers we now have available.

Weather forecasting is notoriously difficult. Supercomputers can be used to create models of conditions in the atmosphere and in the oceans. This capability may help us to predict better severe or violent storms that could cost lives or damage property and crops. In addition, supercomputers may help us to better understand the causes of the increasing size of the hole in the Earth's ozone layer and help us to determine whether there is a warming trend in the Earth's atmosphere.

Supercomputers are used by industries to design advanced materials, more fuel-efficient automobiles, and ever smaller, more powerful microchips. Supercomputers are revolutionizing animation for application both in industries and in entertainment. They make possible the visualization of complex data, creation of virtual reality environments for experimental and educational use, the simulation of space exploration, and storing of vast quantities of accessible information.

Several countries besides the United States are working intensely to develop supercomputers. These include Japan, France, and Germany. On December 10, 1991 President George Bush signed the High Performance Computing Act to accelerate the development of supercomputers and a network to allow them to communicate with work stations at universities, industries, and laboratories throughout the nation. Vice President Albert Gore has promoted a fiber-optic information superhighway to complement the development of supercomputers and to make the information they hold accessible nationwide.

Supercomputer Centers in the United States

In the United States, five supercomputing centers were established by the National Science Foundation (NSF) in 1985. To promote the more efficient use of the computer resources at supercomputer centers, NSF more recently has announced the formation of a

National MetaCenter. A publication from the San Diego Super-computer Center entitled *Computational Science: Advances Through Collaboration* defines the MetaCenter as "a coalescence of intellectual and physical resources unlimited by geographical constraint: a syntheses of individual centers that by combining resources creates a new resource greater than the sum of its parts."

The MetaCenter will combine the resources of four of the NSF supercomputing centers (the San Diego Supercomputing Center, the Cornell Theory Center, the National Center for Supercomputing Applications, and the Pittsburgh Supercomputing Center). A communications network integrates the computational power and human expertise of the four supercomputing centers. Scientists will benefit because they will be able to access a wider range of supercomputer power, perhaps from their own desktop workstations.

Another benefit of the MetaCenter is that it will encourage larger teams of researchers from many interrelated fields of science to work together to solve the most complex and difficult problems known as grand-challenge problems. The MetaCenter also can play a vital part in testing new computer configurations to learn which are most useful and which produce the most valuable kinds of information.

The MetaCenter plans to establish a national file and archival storage system along with a high-speed network dedicated to its use. Files from the national archival storage system will be able to be accessed from the national storage system by local supercomputers. The dedicated network will transfer data within the system linking the four supercomputer centers.

Supercomputer Center Programs

At each NSF supercomputer center, various programs are offered to teachers and students interested in learning more about computers and supercomputers. For example, the San Diego Supercomputing Center (SDSC) has educational programs for students of all ages—from kindergarten to college and even to graduate and postgraduate levels—with workshops, classes, seminars, institutes, tours, and research programs available. The SDSC has the Supercomputing Teacher Enhancement Program (STEP) and a Partnership in Education with the San Diego City Schools Magnet Program. These include activities such as hands-on training sessions for elementary and middle-school teachers, Girl Scout groups, weekend "Discover Science" sessions for teachers, guided tours of the SDSC facility, and a technology checklist for schools to evaluate both the technology available to them and their goals in teaching science.

One of the difficulties to hands-on projects is preparing both the students and the teachers for this interactive kind of learning. STEP helps to prepare high-school math and science teachers with a general understanding of computing and assists them to incorporate computers and computational science into coursework with their students. The first summer of STEP was a three-week workshop for teachers designed to present the tools, concepts, and environments of high-performance computing and computational science.

In a Summer Institute at the National Center for Supercomputing Applications (NCSA) called SuperQuest, high-school students learn about supercomputing and computational science. To be admitted to the program, a team of three or four students and a teacher work together to submit a proposal for a science project that will be conducted on a supercomputer. Project proposals have included a

Children using the supercomputer facility at the San Diego Supercomputer Center on "Kids Day 1993." (Courtesy "Kids Day 1993" at the San Diego Supercomputer Center)

wide selection of topics such as studies of population dynamics, automobile aerodynamics, and predator-prey relationships.

"SuperQuest really broadened my horizon," said Justin Bird, a senior from Berean Academy. "I really didn't understand that supercomputers were more than just fast computers. I realized that this is a whole new world of computing."

Robert Panoff, a SuperQuest mentor and a specialist in computers in education at the North Carolina Supercomputing Center has said, "It's unfortunate that although computers have radically changed the way science is practiced, they haven't yet changed the way science is taught. If teachers are able to use modeling and simulation as examples in the classroom, they have a way of demonstrating scientific principles that the kids can really understand." As another science teacher put it, "One of my students had about ten pages of data. Who can understand ten pages of numbers? Visualization helps with the understanding of the data."

Along with scientific understanding, teacher Jim Zimmerman of Thomas Paine Elementary School, Urbana, Illinois wants to promote global understanding. "We need to challenge ourselves with the idea that we're all teachers and we're all educators in how we act and how we treat others that are different from us. We are all touching the future by what we teach." Zimmerman was one of five teachers from across the country named a Christa McAuliffe Educator by the National Foundation for the Improvement of Education (NFIE) and its Christa McAuliffe Institute for Educational Pioneering. (Christa McAuliffe is the teacher-astronaut who perished in the *Challenger* space mission disaster of January 28, 1986.)

In the five years between 1986 and 1991, the network of supercomputer centers established by the NSF increased the number of researchers who have access to supercomputers over 100 times. Now thousands of scientists from a wide range of fields can use the computational power of supercomputers. As just one example, supercomputers can be used to build a full-scale simulated nuclear-fusion reactor to study results of experimental nuclear-fusion reactions instead of actually building the reactor and performing the experiments.

2

$$\overline{\vee}$$

HOW WERE
SUPERCOMPUTERS
DEVELOPED?

---

*L*ook in a dictionary and you find that one meaning of the word *digit* is finger. When people began to count on their fingers, they were using the world's first "digital computers." The likely reason that our decimal number system is based on the 10 numbers 0 (zero) through 9 is that humans have 10 fingers.

Other ways people have tallied things include scratch marks or notches on wooden sticks and knots on ropes. The ancient Egyptians and Babylonians did calculations by drawing numbers on sand tables and using small pebbles to keep count. (The Latin word *calculus* means "pebble or stone" and is the name given to a branch of mathematics.) The abacus is the equivalent of a portable sand table and is still in use in many parts of the world to do calculations. A person well skilled in the use of the abacus often can match the speed of a hand-held electronic calculator for simple operations such as addition and subtraction.

From Fingers to Mechanical Counting Machines

The development of supercomputers stems from early attempts to build mechanical counting machines. One of the first counting machines was invented by French mathematician and philosopher Blaise Pascal about 1642. The *Pascaline*, as it was called, was about the size of a shoe box and used cogs and gears to do calculations. Though the counter worked, it was too expensive to be successful.

About 30 years later mathematician and inventor Gottfried Leibniz built a device with a large wheellike mechanism that could add, subtract, multiply, and divide. His mechanical counter, the *Leibniz wheel*, was too limited to be truly useful to scientists. However, Leibniz made another important contribution to the development of the computer.

After his death, Leibniz's papers were found to include notes he had written about a number system known as the *binary number system*. Leibniz reasoned that everything in the universe either exists or doesn't exist and can, therefore, be represented using only two numbers, 0 and 1. Leibniz did not complete his work on this new number system, but he had reached the realization that the decimal numbers we use every day can be represented using the two numbers 0 and 1.

Almost two centuries later, in 1854, English mathematician George Boole published his system of Boolean algebra, which stated that everything in the universe could be represented using the numbers 0 and 1. He thought of the numbers 0 and 1 as "nothingness" and "universes." Though the concept of either existing or not existing may seem obvious to us now, this was a revolutionary new advance in thinking about numbers.

Living in England at the same time as George Boole was a mathematician who is aptly called the father of the computer,

BINARY CODE FOR THE ALPHABET

This chart shows how the binary number system, using the American Standard Code for Information Interchange (ASCII-8), represents the letters of the alphabet using only two symbols, 0 (zero) and 1. ASCII-8 is a code that was developed to enable higher-level computer languages to be represented by combinations of the binary numbers 0 and 1 in groups of eight. Each 0 and 1 in the binary number system is called a bit and a group of eight bits is known as a byte. When talking about computers, a word is a group of bits, usually 8 to 64 bits or more in size.

Character	ASCII-8
a	11100001
b	11100010
c	11100011
d	11100100
e	11100101
f	11100110
g	11100111
h	11101000
i	11101001
j	11101010
k	11101011
l	11101100
m	11101101
n	11101110
o	11101111
p	11110000
q	11110001
r	11110010
s	11110011
t	11110100
u	11110101
v	11110110
w	11110111
x	11111000
y	11111001
z	11111010

Portrait of Charles Babbage.
(Courtesy IBM Archives)

Charles Babbage. He designed a mechanical counter, the analytical engine, that had all of the basic parts of a modern computer. The British government was interested in Babbage's idea and supported him with money to build his computing machine. However, after 19 years of effort without results, the government withdrew its financial backing. Though Babbage continued to try to build his machine, the lack of appropriate materials and technologies made successful completion of the project impossible. Babbage was a genius ahead of his time. In 1871 Babbage died—impoverished, discouraged, and without achieving his dream.

Charles Babbage's
analytical engine.
(Courtesy IBM Archives)

Though Babbage may have thought himself a failure, his contributions to modern computer design were a great success. His analytical engine included a "store," which is equivalent to the *memory* in one of today's computers; a "mill," which is likened to the *central processing unit* that actually does the arithmetic; a control unit to guide the sequence of the calculations; an input device to enter information into the machine; and an output device (a typesetting machine) to record answers calculated by the machine.

A New Urgency to Automate Counting—The United States Census

Meanwhile, across the Atlantic Ocean in the United States, the Census Bureau was trying to solve the enormous problem of processing information about the rapidly growing and changing population in the United States. Nearly 10 years after the 1880 census, the data that had been gathered was still not tallied because all of the work was being done by hand. The result was that important information contained in the census was outdated before it could be made available for use.

To tackle this problem, Herman Hollerith designed a machine that used cards with holes punched in them to record information. Each hole in a card represented a fact about an individual such as age, gender, number of children, and whether he or she was married. Hollerith tested his machine using information from a sampling of 10,491 people from four districts in St. Louis who had been included in the 1880 census. Punching the data onto the cards took a little more than 72 hours, but once this task was completed, his machine tabulated the information on the cards in less than six hours; days faster than any competitor's method for handling the census data.

The idea of using punched hole cards originated with Joseph-Marie Jacquard, a French fabric manufacturer. In the early 1880s Jacquard used stiff cards with holes punched into them to program or instruct his looms to weave fabrics with complex patterns. The

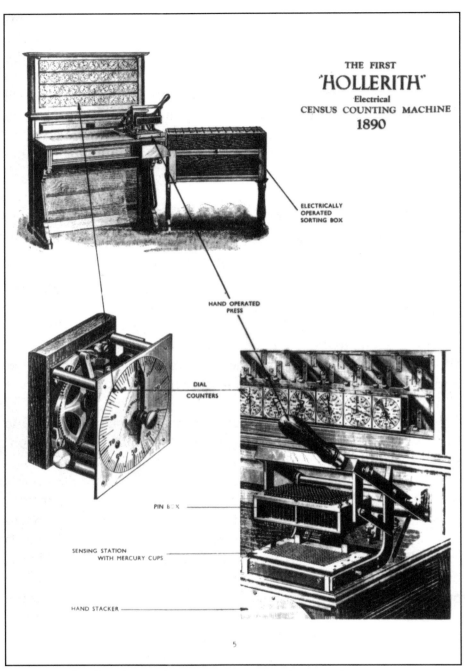

THE FIRST
"HOLLERITH"
Electrical
CENSUS COUNTING MACHINE
1890

ELECTRICALLY
OPERATED
SORTING BOX

HAND OPERATED
PRESS

DIAL
COUNTERS

PIN BOX

SENSING STATION
WITH MERCURY CUPS

HAND STACKER

5

Herman Hollerith's electrical census counting machine, 1890.
(Courtesy IBM Archives)

design woven into the fabric was controlled by altering the pattern of the punched holes in the cards. During the weaving process, a series of rods carried the threads into the loom. At each pass of the shuttle, a single punched hole card blocked some of the rods while it let others slip through to complete one weave of the fabric pattern.

With Hollerith's tabulating machine, all of the data recorded on punched cards could be automatically counted. A stack of cards placed in his machine was processed one card at a time. As each card was counted, a metal plate with hundreds of pins on it pressed against the card. Pins passed through the card wherever there were holes in it and were held back where there were none. Each of the pins that slipped through a hole made contact with a bath of liquid mercury beneath the card, completing an electrical circuit. A needle advanced on a dial and added one more to the total count of the data represented by the hole in the card.

The test with sample data from the 1880 census convinced the U.S. Census Bureau to try Hollerith's tabulating machine to tally the data collected in the 1890 census. The Census Office ordered 56 of Hollerith's tabulators to be delivered to Washington, D.C. The machines were able to complete the 1890 census in only two years, which was an amazing feat for its day.

Hollerith's tabulating machine was so successful that businesses began to buy his machines to automate their offices. Eventually, Hollerith's company grew into a large corporation that merged with other corporations to become International Business Machines (IBM).

The Enormous Early Computers: From Mechanical Relays to Electronic Computing

The burgeoning need to process information and to do long scientific calculations led many individuals besides Herman Hollerith to design machines to speed up the work. One such individual was

Howard Aiken designed the automatic sequence controlled calculator, also known as the Mark I, and it was built by International Business Machines using 3,300 mechanical relays. The computer was dedicated on August 7, 1944. (Courtesy IBM Archives)

Howard Aiken, a graduate student at Harvard University. In order to complete his dissertation for his doctorate, Aiken needed to do an enormous quantity of tedious calculations, and he sought a way to ease the burden. In a memorandum that he wrote in 1937, Aiken proposed to build an automatic calculator from materials that already existed. After finding little support for his machine with several companies, IBM agreed to back the construction of Aiken's computer, the automatic sequence controlled calculator (ASCC), also known as the Mark I.

The Mark I was built at the IBM laboratories in Endicott, New York under the direction of Clair D. Lake and two associates, Franklin D. Hamilton and Benjamin M. Durfee. After a successful test run the Mark I was disassembled and moved to the Cruft Laboratory at Harvard University. Officially dedicated by IBM president Thomas Watson, Sr., on August 7, 1944 the Mark I was the fulfillment of Charles Babbage's vision.

The automatic sequence controlled calculator was 51 feet long and 8 feet high and weighed 5 tons. It consisted of more than 500 miles of wire and about 800,000 parts. Its 3,300 mechanical relays opened and closed, acting like switches turning on and off, to convey the information needed to do calculations. When the Mark I was operating, the opening and closing of the cumbersome relays sounded like the clicking of needles in a roomful of people who were knitting.

The input of instructions for the steps in a calculation and for information for a problem for the Mark I were in the form of punched holes on a continuous paper tape. In addition, about 1,400 rotary switches had to be set before a calculation was run. IBM electric typewriters printed output information. The Mark I could perform three additions every second, which seemed miraculous at the time. During World War II, the need to calculate accurately the trajectories of shells fired from new U.S. Navy guns became urgent. The Mark I was leased by the U.S. Navy Bureau of Ships for the duration of the war and was operated around the clock.

The Mark II succeeded the Mark I, and Howard Aiken designed it still using tried and true mechanical relays. However, one hot day in the summer of 1945, the Mark II suddenly stopped. When the operating crew found the cause of the failure, it discovered a moth that had been crushed to death inside relay #70. The moth was carefully removed with a pair of tweezers and taped into the logbook that was used to record all of the computer's activity. Just then, Howard Aiken entered and asked the crew if they were making any numbers. The crew replied that they were *debugging* the computer, an answer they gave him from then on when the computer was not running. The term *debugging* still is in use, and the logbook with the first "bug" taped in it is kept at the Naval Museum at the Naval Surface Weapons Center in Dahlgren, Virginia.

Even before Howard Aiken designed and built the Mark I and Mark II at Harvard, other advances were underway that affected the development of computers. In the late 1920s a device called the *vacuum tube* was first used as a switch in a computing machine. A vacuum tube looks like an elongated lightbulb with a metal filament inside. Air inside the glass tube is removed, creating a vacuum around the filament. Vacuum tubes were a major advance because they could operate much faster than mechanical relays.

In addition, engineers and others recognized the need for an all-purpose computer—one that could handle many different kinds of calculations and tasks and that would be useful to businesses as well as scientists. American physicists John Mauchly and J. Presper Eckert built one of the first electronic computers, the Electronic Numerical Integrator and Calculator, or ENIAC, at the University of Pennsylvania.

ENIAC, the first electronic general-purpose computer, was built during the latter years of World War II. It was capable of doing complex mathematical calculations as well as the more routine financial figuring needed by businesses such as banks. ENIAC was a huge behemoth of more than 100 feet long and 10 feet high and weighed more than 30 tons. The computer housed over 18,000 glass electronic vacuum tubes and took more than two and one-half years to construct.

When ENIAC was finally ready in 1946, it showed off its capabilities. It could compute the trajectory of an artillery shell in only 20 seconds; this was faster than the 30 seconds the shell took to reach its target. Once, ENIAC solved a difficult equation requiring 15 million multiplications in only one weekend. The same calculations were equivalent to approximately 40 years of work by a person using a desktop calculator. At a public demonstration, ENIAC multiplied 97,367 by itself 5,000 times in less than half a second, prompting a news reporter to describe its operation as

The Electronic Numerical Integrator and Calculator, or ENIAC, was one of the first electronic computers and was built by John Mauchly and J. Presper Eckert. The computer contained more than 18,000 electronic vacuum tubes. (Courtesy Apple Computer, Inc.)

An array of electron vacuum tubes is shown in a photograph taken about 1944.
(Courtesy AT&T Bell Laboratories)

"faster than thought." The ENIAC was 1,000 times faster than a human using an abacus.

However, ENIAC was not without problems. Its power-hungry vacuum tubes generated a tremendous amount of heat. When some of them failed, the computer could not be used until troubleshooters located and replaced the defective tubes—a costly and time-consuming task.

The Tale of the Incredible Shrinking Computers

Though computers such as the Mark I and ENIAC were considered to be modern miracles for their time, they were expensive, gargantuan in size, and prone to the failure of mechanical relays, loose wires, or overheated, breakable glass vacuum tubes.

These problems were largely solved by a revolutionary new advance that would quickly replace relays and vacuum tubes as switching devices in computers. Scientists William Shockley, Walter Brattain, and John Bardeen developed the *transistor* at Bell Laboratories in 1948. This "solid-state" electronic device was only about the size of a pencil eraser, and 200 of them could fit in the same space as one vacuum tube. In addition, a transistor is a much more

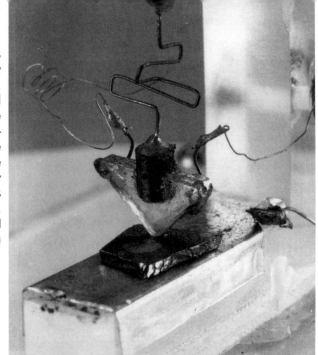

The first transistors assembled by William Shockley, Walter Brattain, and John Bardeen were primitive in appearance, but they were destined to revolutionize the electronics industry and the way computers were built. (Courtesy AT&T Bell Laboratories)

reliable switch than a relay or vacuum tube. The amount of energy needed to operate a transistor and the amount of heat generated by a transistor are far less than for a vacuum tube.

Transistors operate at significantly faster speeds than relays or vacuum tubes do. ENIAC was a *first-generation computer*. It could compute at speeds of 1,000 to 5,000 additions per second. However, computers built with transistors were *second-generation computers* that could operate at speeds as high as 500,000 additions per second.

Transistors are made from silicon, a material found in ordinary sand. Silicon is a *semiconductor*. A *conductor*, such as a metal, allows electricity to flow through it easily. An *insulator*, such as rubber, does not allow electricity to flow through it. However, a semiconductor, as its name implies, is somewhere in between. It neither allows electricity to flow through it easily, nor does it entirely stop the flow of electricity, and if small amounts of certain impurities are added to silicon, the flow of electricity through it can be controlled.

The three Bell Labs scientists won the Nobel Prize in Physics in 1956 for their invention of the transistor and for their discovery that the flow of electricity through a silicon transistor could be controlled and thus act as a switch that is either ON or OFF, just as with a vacuum tube. Most of the computers using transistors were built between the late 1950s and 1964.

In addition to the discoveries of scientists, another impetus was shaping the future of computers. In October 1957 the Soviet Union triumphantly put the first artificial satellite, *Sputnik*, into orbit around the Earth. The event launched the USSR and the United States into a space race. The United States was determined to regain technological superiority.

Transistors were a revolutionary advance in the building of computers. But despite the advantages made possible by this scientific breakthrough, even faster and lighter-weight computers were needed to go into space successfully. In addition, transistors still needed to be hand wired together onto circuit boards, the wires that connected them were large and cumbersome in comparison to the size of the transistors, and the wire connections sometimes failed. The idea of manufacturing miniature transistors connected together on a single piece of silicon became a new goal for reducing the size and weight of computers and for increasing their efficiency and reliability.

Integrated Circuits and Microchips

In the late 1950s Jack Kilby tackled this problem while he was working at Texas Instruments. He devised a way to manufacture miniature electronic transistors on a single silicon chip and applied for a patent for his *integrated circuits* (ICs) in February 1959. Kilby's ICs reduced transistors to the size of a match head. However, the transistors on the silicon chip still needed to be wired together.

Meanwhile, another scientist was at work on the same problem at another company, Fairchild Semiconductor. Robert Noyce invented an IC in which the transistors on the chip were connected not by wires, but by tiny lines of metal printed and imbedded directly into the silicon of the chip during the manufacturing process. In this kind of integrated circuit, the transistors and electrical connections were all one piece. This one-piece IC proved to be much more efficient and reliable than ICs with transistors that were wired together by hand. Noyce filed for a patent on his IC only five months after Jack Kilby. Integrated circuits made possible the *third generation* of computers.

The first integrated circuits were available on the market by the spring of 1961. In May President John F. Kennedy vowed to put an American astronaut on the moon by the end of the decade. Following the president's announcement, NASA chose to use Robert Noyce's ICs for the computers on their spacecraft. In June 1968 Noyce left Fairchild Semiconductor to found his own company, Intel, and on July 20, 1969 astronaut Neil Armstrong fulfilled the national mission as the first human to set foot on the surface of the moon.

Once integrated circuits were invented, competitors raced to put more and more components onto a single chip, and the numbers kept increasing. In 1964 10 transistor circuits were on a chip. By 1969, with the capability to do large-scale integration, or LSI, there was a hundredfold jump to 1,000 transistors and other components on a single chip. With large-scale integration came the *fourth generation* of computers. They were smaller, faster, and more reliable than ever before.

In 1969 Intel employee Ted Hoff designed a chip that had all of the components of the central processing unit (CPU) of a computer. The tiny size of the components and their arrangement within the chip made possible a "computer on a chip," also known as a *microprocessor*. Hoff's new microprocessor contained 2,300 transistors and measured just $1/8$ inch by $1/6$ inch, but, amazingly, its power was equivalent to ENIAC's. By 1971, the first microprocessor was available.

Manufacturing Microchips

When you consider the miniature size of a microchip, it is hard to imagine how it is made. A chip may be as small as $1/8$ inch on a side and only as thick as your fingernail. Yet, a chip tiny enough to pass through the eye of a sewing needle may contain more than a million circuit lines and transistors.

The making of microchips is one of the most complex manufacturing processes known. Silicon is melted and then hardened into a boule, a solid long crystal, usually about 3 or 4 inches in diameter and up to several feet long. The crystal is shaped and polished and then sliced into thin wafers.

Each wafer is polished to a mirror-smooth finish on one side. The wafer then is heated with oxygen in a special high-temperature oven. During this treatment, a microscopically thin layer of silicon dioxide, or glass, forms on the surface of the wafer. The glass layer acts as an insulator.

Engineers design the circuits and other electronic devices such as transistors that are to be formed on each chip. Their designs are

A MIPS R 8000 chip set. Despite their tiny size, these microchips are as powerful as some of the Cray supercomputer models. (Image courtesy of MIPS Technologies, Inc., a subsidiary of Silicon Graphics, Inc.)

photographically reduced until they are small enough to be used to make the microchip. A mask is made with the design for one chip repeated on it in columns and rows so that hundreds of identical microchips can be manufactured on one wafer of silicon. The mask is used like a stencil over the silicon wafer, which is treated to harden only the exposed portions of its surface. Later, chemicals wash away the unhardened portions of each chip on the surface of the wafer.

Now the hardened areas of the wafer coating are washed away and treated with substances called dopants to alter the silicon so that it will conduct electricity. Layers of transistors and circuits are added in a similar manner, forming thousands of transistors and circuits on each microchip on the wafer.

After a wafer full of microchips is finished, each chip on the wafer is tested to make sure it is working properly. Then the wafer is cut into hundreds of microchips.

A large computer may have many kinds of chips inside. Some of them are part of the storage system, some control the input and output devices, and some are part of the central processing unit. The miniaturization process is so refined that all of the transistors, wires, and other components necessary for a computer can fit onto one silicon chip that is smaller than a fingernail. The "computer-on-a-chip," or microprocessor, has found many uses and is inside video games, calculators, digital watches, industrial robots, and automobiles with "cruise control," among other places.

Microprocessors have made possible calculators more power-ful than ENIAC that fit in the palm of your hand and personal computers that are inexpensive enough for widespread home use.

With very large-scale integration, or VLSI, the goal in the mid-1970s was to put 32,000 circuits on a chip; more recently the number of components on a chip is at the million mark. The extraordinary miniaturization of microchips with VLSI has made possible the building of the first supercomputers. Now the MIPS R 8000 chip set is the world's fastest supercomputing microproc-essor. The MIPS R 8000 microchip has computational perform-ance nearly equivalent to a CRAY Y-MP supercomputer.

3

SEYMOUR CRAY AND THE FIRST SUPERCOMPUTERS

*I*n 1925 in Chippewa Falls, Wisconsin Seymour Cray was born. Cray was one of the first people to dedicate himself to the development of supercomputers. After he received a bachelor's degree in electrical engineering from the University of Minnesota in 1950, he spent a year studying applied mathematics and completed a master's degree in 1951. Cray worked for Engineering Research Associates (ERA) and then for Remington Rand and Sperry Rand. Seymour Cray was interested in software, logic, and circuit design. The first computer he designed was a scientific computer, the ERA 1101. He also did a lot of the design work on the UNIVAC 1103 computer.

Seymour Cray Founds a Supercomputer Company

Cray and several other scientists left Sperry Rand in 1957 to found a new company, Control Data Corporation (CDC). Seymour Cray decided to build a solid-state supercomputer using printed circuits and transistors rather than vacuum tubes. In less than two years Control Data Corporation announced the CDC 1604 computer. It could do high-speed calculations with great accuracy and cost less than other similar computers. Moreover, it made Seymour Cray famous.

The success of the computer also meant that CDC had become a growing company. However, Seymour Cray's main interest was to build the fastest computers, not to administer the everyday business workings of a company. He decided to leave Control Data Corporation but was asked to stay. He agreed but only if he could work from his hometown of Chippewa Falls. CDC built a laboratory for Cray near his hometown and within walking distance of his house. Cray became a recluse who secluded himself from his business associates and whose sole interest was to build the world's best supercomputers.

Build them he did. Rumor had it that Cray built his computers on a card table on the porch of his home, using tweezers and a

Seymour Cray with the CRAY-2 supercomputer. (Courtesy Cray Research, Inc.)

soldering gun. But what he really used was a pencil and a pad of 8½-by-11-inch paper each day. With these simple tools, Cray did the necessary calculations, had them checked by a team of 30 or more people on the development team, and then had workers assemble computer chips into a module of the computer.

The CDC 6600 computer was announced on August 22, 1963 and was the most powerful computer ever built until that time—three times more powerful than STRETCH, a computer IBM had stopped building a few years earlier. The CDC 6600 made CDC a leader in the industry. By computer standards, at $7.5 million, the CDC 6600 was significantly less costly than other high-speed computers.

The CDC 6600 computer was built with transistors that were so densely packed that a freon cooling system was necessary to keep the components from overheating. The customer for the computer was the U.S. Atomic Energy Commission (AEC). The CDC 6600 was delivered to the AEC Livermore Laboratory in February 1964. The computer contained 350,000 transistors and took six months to debug.

By 1967, 63 CDC 6600 computers were in use. Most were owned by government agencies such as the AEC or by large corporations. Meanwhile, Seymour Cray continued to design and build more powerful supercomputers. In 1969 the CDC 7600 was introduced. It was followed by the CDC 8600, but Control Data Corporation did not market this model.

The Making of Another New Company

When the emphasis at Control Data Corporation shifted to commercial computers rather than scientific computers, Seymour Cray decided once again to make a change and in 1972 founded Cray Research, a company dedicated solely to building supercomputers.

The first supercomputer built by Cray Research was the CRAY-1. Because of its computing capabilities, many people considered it to be the first true supercomputer. The CRAY-1 was 6

The CRAY-1 supercomputer was considered to be the first true supercomputer. It was built using more than 200,000 computer chips. (Courtesy Cray Research, Inc.)

feet high and 8 feet in diameter. Its components included more than 200,000 computer chips, 60 miles of wiring, and 3,400 integrated circuit boards. It was purchased by the Los Alamos National Laboratory and installed in the spring of 1976.

The CRAY-1 was innovative and unique in many ways. The most striking design feature of the computer was its revolutionary circular shape. Seymour Cray had created the new design to enable him to limit the length of the wires connecting the components inside the computer to a maximum of 4 feet. Limiting the length of the connecting wires significantly increased the speed of operation of the computer.

In an ideal conductor (such as a *superconductor* that shows no electrical resistance), electricity travels at the speed of light (186,000 miles per second or 299,793 kilometers per second), which would be about 1 foot per *nanosecond* (a nanosecond is one billionth of a second). But the actual speed of electricity passing through wires is slower, and because the switches in a computer take only about one nanosecond to operate, the time it takes for electricity to travel within the wire connectors slows the computer's operation. The longer the distance electricity must travel within the wires, the greater the operating time lost.

The CRAY-1 was the first supercomputer to offer an effective way to work on more than one part of a computer problem at the same time. By using a concept known as *vector processing*, a single operation such as multiplication can be performed simultaneously on a whole list of numbers. The CRAY-1 was capable of processing 1 million 64-bit words and had an *operating clock speed* (the smallest interval of time in which synchronized operations take place within a computer) of 12.5 nanoseconds.

By 1979, Cray Research announced that it would build the CRAY-2. This supercomputer was expected to be four to six times more powerful than its predecessor. The CRAY-2 was housed in a C-shaped cabinet packed with 240,000 computer chips. With this design, the maximum length of each portion of connecting wiring used was reduced to 16 inches. The CRAY-2 had the largest available internal memory with a capacity of 2 billion bytes, and it could process 1.2 billion floating-point operations, or flops, per second. Its components include four processors that can be run together to make the CRAY-2 up to 12 times faster than the CRAY-1.

The CRAY-2 had 256 million words of central memory compared to the CRAY-1's 1 million. The CRAY-2 also was smaller than the CRAY-1, measuring only 53 inches in diameter and 45 inches in height. Its reduced size meant that its components were tightly packed into its design, so much so that the CRAY-2 needed to be cooled in a unique way. The circuits of the CRAY-2 were bathed in a liquid coolant, prompting one scientist to refer to it as "a computer in an aquarium." But the payoff of its innovative design was that the CRAY-2 had an operating clock speed of only 4 nanoseconds. It could do in one second what took scientists one year to accomplish as recently as 1952. The first CRAY-2 was sold to the Lawrence Livermore National Laboratory in Livermore, California.

In April 1982 Cray Research announced a new series of computer systems, the CRAY X-MP. These were the first CRAY computers that Seymour Cray had not designed entirely by himself. They were designed instead by Steve Chen, and they improved upon the CRAY-1. The CRAY X-MP was 10 times faster than the original CRAY-1 and could do 1 billion operations per second. This was twice as fast as any Japanese supercomputers. Cray Research sold about 50 of the CRAY X-MP supercomputers by the spring of 1985.

Seymour Cray said of himself, "I do tend to look forward in my thinking, and I don't like to rest on my laurels." So Seymour Cray continued to design ever faster and more-powerful supercomputers. The CRAY-3 has 16 processors and an 8-billion-byte memory. It was built using galium arsenide computer chips because they operate about 10 times faster than chips made with silicon. (The disadvantage to galium arsenide is that the material is more brittle than silicon. For this reason galium arsenide computer chips are more difficult to manufacture than silicon chips.) The longest wire used to connect the components in the CRAY-3 is 3 inches. People have called the CRAY-3 the "breadbox computer" because it is only one-fifth the size of the CRAY-2.

High-Tech Chess and Checkers

An interesting area of supercomputer usage that combines science and fun is the competition between computers playing chess. The game of chess uses logic and follows specific rules. Carnegie-Mellon University developed HITECH, a special-purpose computer that took part in a chess competition with a CRAY X-MP/48 (general-purpose) computer chess team called Cray Blitz. At the North American Computer Chess Championship matches in October 1985, the HITECH computer won. But in June 1986 in Cologne, Germany, the Cray Blitz team won the World Computer Chess Championship, a title it had previously captured in 1983.

These chess competitions may seem frivolous, but they are not idle games. Chess programs must be capable of looking ahead at possible future moves. For example, the Cray Blitz program can

The CRAY X-MP/4 systems offer 10 times the performance of the CRAY-1 supercomputer and feature four identical central processing units. In the background of the CRAY X-MP/4 is the X-MP's input/output subsystem, and in the foreground is a solid-state storage device. (Courtesy Cray Research, Inc.)

anticipate up to eight moves ahead and look at approximately 100,000 different chess-board positions each second. The HITECH has a similar capability. These same characteristics are valuable learning tools in solving many scientific problems.

In addition to computers playing chess, a checkers competition took place in August 1994 between a supercomputer named Chinook and the top-seeded checkers player in the world, Marion Tinsley, at the Computer Museum in Boston, Massachusetts. Chinook can assess 12 million potential moves per second. So far, despite the supercomputer's formidable capacity, whenever Chinook and Tinsley have played checkers, the retired mathematics professor from Georgia has won or had a draw with the computer. Unfortunately, Professor Tinsley had to stop playing on orders from his physician due to ill health.

4
$\overline{\vee}$

PARALLEL PROCESSING SPEEDS COMPUTERS INTO THE FUTURE

P*arallel processing* is the execution of several operations or several parts of an operation on a computer at the same time. The term applies to computers that have more than one processor or even a very large number of processors.

Mass-producing Calculations

Parallel processing is a new way of arranging the component parts of a computer, also known as its architecture, to allow the computer to work on many portions of a problem or calculation simultaneously.

A comparison can be made between this new computer architecture and the advent of mass production in the Industrial Revolution.

In the 1790s Congress wanted to encourage manufacturers to start to produce military firearms in the United States. At the time, the United States was in danger of going to war with the French, and most of the rifles used by American militiamen were being imported from France. Congress allotted funds for 20,000 rifles. The quantity seemed staggering because in those days all firearms were individually made by hand and the most a factory could turn out was a few hundred guns each year. In addition to the traditional method of production being painfully slow, each rifle was slightly different from all others, and if repairs were needed, the parts would need to be custom-made to fit the particular rifle.

Eli Whitney, the inventor of the cotton gin, won a contract from the U.S. government to build thousands of rifles. He proposed the idea of manufacturing guns with interchangeable parts. He would use templates to produce large batches of parts that were all alike. The method that Eli Whitney devised, called mass production, is now used to manufacture all large volume goods. Mass production of rifles not only revolutionized the manufacture of goods, but it also meant that if a firearm needed repair, a new part could be obtained that would fit perfectly without the need to customize it.

Mass production organized the manufacturing process so as to make possible the manufacture of large quantities of previously unattainable goods at a price many people could afford. The key to this accomplishment was to do more than one thing at once. In a similar way, parallel processing organizes how information is processed to do more than one thing at once and so to produce calculations or solutions to problems as quickly and efficiently as possible. Just as mass-produced goods may be manufactured in batches, information or data can be simultaneously processed to speed the answers to problems.

There are several ways in which parallel processing is handled. One method of parallel processing is called *pipelining* and resembles the sequence of operations in an assembly line. With pipelining, several computer operations may occur at the same time, such as readying data, calculating sums, and storing results from previous operations. This is the same way that vector computers operate.

Another technique of parallel processing is *functional parallelism*. This method can be compared to building an item, such as a washing machine, using several assembly lines. The outer housing of the machine is built on one assembly line, while the porcelain-coated tub and the motor are readied on other assembly lines. Each operation is kept separate until the tub and the motor are placed inside the housing of the washing machine. Functional parallelism allows separate parts of the computer to operate simultaneously on portions of the data needed to solve a problem. Later, the resultant data can be integrated to reach an answer.

Both of these techniques, pipelining and functional parallelism, speed up computation, but in each case many different operations are being performed at once and if a problem consists of 12 steps, no more than 12 steps can be done simultaneously.

With another technique called *data parallelism*, the computer does the same operation on many portions of the data for a problem concurrently. This method allows the rate of processing to be increased by factors that are determined by the amount of data to processed, not by the number of steps in an operation. The important distinction with data parallelism is that the more data there is to be processed, the greater the potential is for increasing the rate at which the data can be processed. This means that a computer with parallel architecture may be able to process two or three times as much data in the same length of time by adding extra processors to do the job.

Why Is Parallel Processing Important?

During the years of the development of computers, there were rapid improvements in the speed with which computers could carry out calculations. First, mechanical computers built with gears or relays were replaced by machines that operated with electronic vacuum tubes and, although the tubes were not as reliable as relays, their switching speed was much faster. Then transistors produced a breakthrough leading to a quantum leap in lower costs, reliability, and speed of operation. The invention of the integrated circuit and the very large scale integrated microchip brought us into the modern era of nanosecond computer operations. However, the numbers of transistors and circuits that can be squeezed onto a single silicon chip may be reaching its physical limits, and new approaches to increasing the speed of operations of computers are needed.

Until recently, most computers were built following the von Neumann model, an architecture devised by one of the world's foremost mathematicians, John von Neumann. In the 1940s, von Neumann wrote a draft of a paper describing the logic and makeup of the EDVAC, a high-speed automatic digital computer that had a stored, programmable memory. The model he described utilized one central processor to do all of the operations to solve a calculation. Each of the operations was performed serially, one after another, in a sequence of single steps. There was much passing back and forth of data between the computer's single processor and the memory.

Increasing the speed of computer operation by using several processors, each working on one part of a problem simultaneously with the other processors, has been compared to the output of a single-piston internal combustion engine and one that has four, six, or more cylinders. Though the programs needed to run several processors at one time are more complex, interest in using this method to achieve faster computing has blossomed. For example, the CRAY X-MP is available with one, two, or four processors. The CRAY-2 may have two processors or four, and there are up to eight processors in the ETA-10 supercomputer.

Some supercomputers, such as the CRAYs, use only a few full-scale processors. These are called *coarse-grained systems*. Supercomputers that use large numbers of less-powerful processors are called *fine-grained systems*. Thinking Machines Corporation in Cambridge, Massachusetts makes what may be viewed as an ultra fine-grained computer system. It has 64,000 processors and each one processes one bit of information at a time. Another computer company, Floating Point Systems (FPS) offers identical computer modules that can be bought in quantities of a few processors to more than 16,000 processors configured into a parallel processing computer.

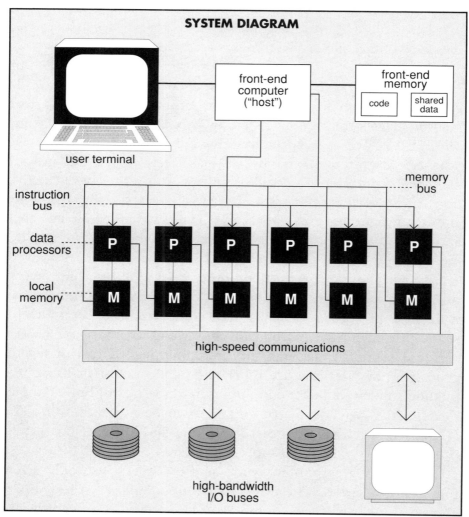

Figure 1 This diagram depicts a Connection Machine system with multiple processors. The user communicates with a "host" computer using a conventional computer terminal and language. The "host" computer delegates operations to the parallel processors, where they are done in parallel, at the same time, rather than in a series of operations, one after another.

This Thinking Machines Connection Machine, CM-2, with Data Vault is located at the National Center for Supercomputing Applications. (Courtesy National Center for Supercomputing Applications)

One important point to recognize is that the speed of operation of a multiple-processor computer does not multiply proportionally with the number of processors in the machine. For example, tests done at Lawrence Livermore National Laboratory show improvements in performance of about 3.7 times with computers with four processors. One reason for this is that a computer must coordinate the information that is being exchanged within its components. This means that part of the time a processor is communicating with the computer's other processors rather than working on the numbers needed to solve a problem or calculation. In addition, some processors may complete their tasks and then have to wait for data from another processor, decreasing computer speed and efficiency.

The human brain is a model of an extremely efficient parallel processing system. Communication among the parts of the human brain are so efficient that it is difficult to imagine duplicating its power with an electronic device or machine. However, designers are trying to emulate the human brain's achievements. One method is a high-speed switching system. Switching speeds that run at 32 million bits per second are found in computers like the Butterfly from Bolt, Beranek & Newman, Inc. (BBN). In addition, various features can be designed into the way the components of a computer are configured and linked together to improve the computer's internal communications.

Another problem with parallel processing is that *operating systems* are not standardized. Occam is a standardized operating system that was developed at Oxford University in 1983. It can be used on any system of processors, whether they are operating in parallel or serially as in the classic von Neumann model. Floating Point Systems uses Occam as a standard item with its T-series of computers. Scientists at Cornell University also are working toward standardization of an operating system for the T-series.

In addition, programmers at National Science Foundation supercomputer centers, national laboratories, and universities are working toward *compilers* that will enable programs in the scientific computer language FORTRAN to be used on parallel processor supercomputers. A *compiler* is a computer program that translates the instructions in a symbolic language such as FORTRAN into machine language that the computer can understand and use.

Local Area Networks, Hypercomputers, and Linda

An example of another way for many companies to access the equivalent of supercomputer power is to connect the processors of their already existent workstation desktop personal computers into a local area network (LAN). As an example, assume that a network of 20 workstation personal computers exists and that during the workday, the computers' processors are idle as much as half of the time. Effectively, this means that the company owns a 10-processor parallel computer if it can access the free time of each of the personal computer's processors. This kind of network-based parallel computer system is known as a *hypercomputer*. It is useful when supercomputer power is needed only occasionally by any one of the connected personal computers.

With a hypercomputer, a difficult problem can be broken into smaller pieces, and one piece can be handed to each of several processors. The processors may be located anywhere and their processing capability is shared by many personal computers. This networking arrangement of shared processors has the advantage of making use of any idle processor capacity. It is almost like having a parallel processor supercomputer genie emerge from the computer network that a company already owns.

Appropriate software is needed to use a hypercomputer. One example of a coordinating parallel computer language is the software called Linda, which was developed by David Gelernter,

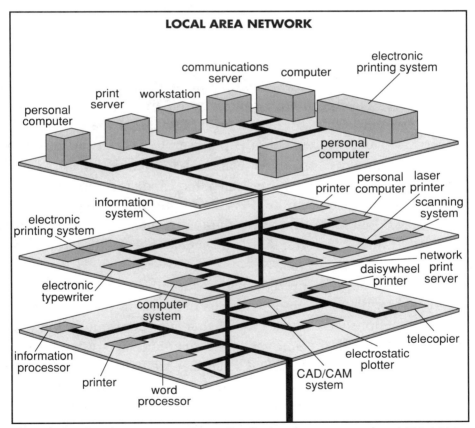

Figure 2 This diagram is an example of a local area network or LAN. LANs allow multiple workstations within an office or building to communicate with each other and to share common resources.

Nicholas Carriero, Jerrold Leichter, and others at Yale University. Linda allows companies to utilize the hypercomputer capacity of their personal computer networks.

Parallel programs for hypercomputers such as Linda don't know which processors they will be run on, and they don't know how many processors will be available to run a particular program. They must be able to take advantage of any processors that are available whenever they are available. Linda accomplishes this by using *tuple space*.

Tuple space is a kind of shared memory in which the items in the memory have no address. In effect, this means that any task (each task is called a tuple) in tuple space can be accessed without regard to its physical location or the order of the items. Tuple space holds the input data that has been entered as well as intermediate results from operations that have already been completed. This dynamic freedom of access is compatible with the hypercomputer architecture. The speed with which a problem is solved depends upon how many processors work on it. The larger the number of processors available, the faster the program works out the answer.

In experiments at Sandia National Laboratories, up to 13 processors linked together have shown that Linda is flexible enough to compete favorably with a CRAY computer on some problems. Also, AT&T Bell Laboratories has built a parallel processing computer, the Linda Machine, that is designed specifically to use the tuple-space software Linda.

A hypercomputer needs a way to distribute the tasks to be performed by the processors within its network of those available. This is accomplished using a process that runs continuously in the background called the *daemon*. The daemon has two parts, a scheduler and an allocator. The scheduler waits for processors in the network to become available, and the allocator sends a message to the scheduler if a processor in the network is available for use.

Hypercomputers utilize otherwise-wasted computer power in a way that may prove economical for companies that already have invested in personal computer networks.

∇

5

THE STRUCTURE OF A SUPERCOMPUTER SYSTEM

*I*n July 1984 the National Science Foundation (NSF) initiated a drive to make the computational power of supercomputers more easily available to scientists and researchers. To encourage the development and growth of supercomputers, several existing supercomputer installations were funded by the NSF. These included facilities at Purdue University, University of Minnesota, and Boeing Computer Services. Added later were Colorado State University, Digital Productions in Los Angeles, and AT&T Bell Laboratories. Researchers unfamiliar with supercomputing could try different models of supercomputers, such as the CRAY 1/A and 1/S, the CRAY-2, the CRAY X-MP, and the Cyber 205, that were installed at these locations.

The NSF formed the Office of Advanced Scientific Computing in 1985, which made available 22,000 hours of supercomputer time for researchers and other users. Next, the NSF sought proposals for review and then selected five projects for funding. These were the Center for Theory and Simulation in Science and Engineering at Cornell University (often shortened to Cornell Theory Center), the National Center for Supercomputing Applications (NCSA) at the University of Illinois at Champaign/Urbana, the Pittsburgh Supercomputer Center (PSC), the John von Neumann Center for Scientific Computing (JVNC) at Princeton, New Jersey, and the San Diego Supercomputer Center (SDSC) at the University of California, San Diego.

The centers at San Diego, Cornell, and Princeton have participants throughout the United States, and those affiliated with San Diego's Supercomputer Center cover a range of locations from Maryland to Hawaii. By the spring of 1987, more than 100 universities and other users were participating.

Although no one supercomputer represents all installations, the supercomputer at the San Diego Supercomputer Center is an example of how one supercomputer is set up, or configured. A company named GA Technologies, Inc., came up with the idea for the SDSC and now it manages the center. The SDSC can work on a large number of different problems at once by using a time-sharing process.

The San Diego Supercomputing Center is one of five supercomputer centers in the United States that were selected to be funded by the National Science Foundation in 1985. (Courtesy San Diego Supercomputing Center)

Brain of the Supercomputer:
The Central Processing Unit

The central processing unit (CPU) at the SDSC originally was a CRAY X-MP/48, which consisted of four CPUs with a single active memory of 8 million 64-bit words. The "words" represented numbers as well as other symbols in binary code. The *operating clock speed*, or basic speed at which the computer operated, was 8.5 nanoseconds, giving the supercomputer enormous capacity to tackle problems.

However, in October 1993 SDSC's main production supercomputer was updated with a CRAY C98/8128 supercomputing system. The system includes eight processors with a cycle time of 4 nanoseconds per processor. The main memory has a capacity of 128 million words or 1 gigabyte (the prefix *giga-* means 1 billion). Also, there is solid-state storage capacity of 512 million words or 4 gigabytes. Additional local storage capacity is 150 gigabytes.

In order to maintain high-speed computing, a large active memory is needed to handle the long, difficult programs and problems. The supercomputer must store input data as well as computations that are under way and then be able to pick them up again when they are needed. Some supercomputers such as one at the National Center for Atmospheric Research have a solid-state storage device (SSD) made up of a large grouping of computer chips linked to the CPU to provide extra memory.

SDSC has two parallel processing systems. One of them is the Intel Paragon, and the other is an nCUBE 2. To provide long-term storage of data at SDSC for CRAY, Paragon, and nCUBE users, there is a system with 120 GBytes of disk space and more than 6 trillion bytes (TBytes) of cartridge tape storage. Disk and cartridge-tape storage are ways to store computer data as variations in magnetization. The information on disks and tapes can be erased and later replaced with new data.

When most researchers and scientists want to access the supercomputer capability at SDSC, they can use NSFnet, the network set up by the National Science Foundation, which is part of the Internet; other networks; or direct-dial telephone.

The Internet consists of the millions of computers all over the world that are connected to each other and can pass on information or share computer files no matter where they are. Originally, the Internet began as an experiment to see if a disaster-proof computer system could be created that would allow U.S. scientists or military personnel to communicate with their colleagues no matter where they were located. The original project was called ARPAnet (ARPA stands for Advanced Research Projects Agency), and it gradually grew to include networks such as NSFnet, NASA Science Internet, and many other networks.

The Internet is loosely organized, and no one person or group oversees its operation. Today, people can find almost any kind of information they are seeking on the Internet. For example, businesses interested in international trade can look up information contained in the General Agreement on Tariffs and Trade or in the North American Free Trade Agreement. They also can get up-to-date demographic statistics, economic news, or consumer information.

The Internet can be accessed through any of the connected networks that are part of it. Universities and many large companies have direct connections to the Internet, most often through sources such as Performance Systems International (PSI), a major provider of this service. The Internet also can be accessed through dial-up providers with whom you establish an account. The dial-up providers access the Internet through their computers. There also are commercial services available to connect your own computer to the Internet such as America Online, CompuServe, GEnie, and Prodigy.

Programs:
Instructions for the Supercomputer

Without a set of instructions, no computer, not even a supercomputer, can operate. *Programs* are instructions that direct a computer to perform the tasks necessary to solve a problem or to analyze or store data. Supercomputers are usually used to solve the most complex problems and, therefore, the design of the programs needed to operate them are of vital importance and must enhance their performance.

The *operating program*, or *system*, oversees or manages the workings of the computer itself. The operating system is adapted to enhance the characteristics or architecture of a particular type of computer. For example, most IBM-compatible personal computers use Microsoft MS-DOS as their operating system. (*DOS* stands for "disk operating system.")

In addition to operation systems, there are *applications programs* that instruct the computer to do specific tasks. For example, if you have an IBM-compatible personal computer with the Microsoft MS-DOS operating system, you still need additional software programs to do tasks such as accounting or word processing. Two applications programs or software for word processing are Word-Perfect and Microsoft Word. Business accounting can be done with a computer using applications programs such as DAC-Easy and M.Y.O.B. There are many other applications programs that perform these functions, and the user must choose the software best suited to his or her word-processing or business-accounting needs. Programs also exist for innumerable tasks such as keeping track of personal finances and checking accounts, creating mailing lists and labels, generating computer graphics, and playing with computer games.

Scientists often must adapt applications programs to suit their own needs for a particular research problem. For example, some computer languages have been in use for long periods of time. FORTRAN has been around since 1957 and is still the most-used language for scientific problems. Because so many people are familiar with FORTRAN and because so much work has been done using it, FORTRAN can not be easily replaced with something entirely new.

To assist researchers in their work, supercomputer centers make available to users various applications software to perform certain specific kinds of calculations or tasks. These applications programs were developed by other scientists at laboratories and universities all over the world or by private companies. Some of the areas of study that have applications programs available at the SDSC include biology, chemistry, electrical engineering, graphics, mathematics, mechanics, and nuclear engineering.

When computers are used to study scientific problems, the process is called computational science. Supercomputers are capable of performing more mathematics per second and can evaluate more information than less-powerful computers. Supercomputers also can create more-detailed and accurate models to help researchers better visualize solutions to problems. Supercomputer power is essential to study many of the most fundamental problems of science, economics, and society. These principal topics of scientific research have been called grand-challenge problems.

Understanding and answering grand-challenge problems are essential to the well-being of all people on planet Earth. To give an idea of the scope of some of the grand challenges, a few of them are: to assess accurately and clean up the pollution of our air and water; to find treatments for diseases such as Alzheimer's and AIDS; and to be better able to predict severe earthquakes or long-term changes in climate.

Memory:
A Place to Store Data and Instructions

Data and instructions needed for calculations or problem solving are stored in a computer's *memory*. If a computer has more than one processor, each processor may have its own memory and may, in addition, share a central memory with the other processors. A supercomputer has a place to store information that is needed for immediate use as well as a place to store more permanent information that may be needed in the future.

The CRAY X-MP/48 supercomputer at San Diego has an active memory of 8 million 64-bit words. In addition, there are 12 CRAY DD-49s that store short-term information magnetically on disks. Information on these disks is quickly accessible for computations and can be transferred back and forth to the central processing unit at very high speed, 10 million bits per second. The storage disks are stacked to create a compact memory device with a capacity of 15 gigabytes (a gigabyte is 1 billion bytes).

An IBM 4381 computer also manages an additional on-line storage capacity of 50 gigabytes of disk memory. However, even with this enormous capability, the information stored on these disks must be saved elsewhere by the user within 36 hours or it will be erased automatically to avoid cluttering the storage system.

The IBM 4381 computer also stores more permanent, inactive information and off-line data on cassettes that resemble video-cassettes. The cassettes have replaced reels of magnetic tape that previously had been used for long-term storage at the San Diego Supercomputer Center.

I/O:
The Input and Output of Information

Because of the high volume of data and their high speeds of operation, supercomputers need other computers to oversee the *input* and *output* of information. The San Diego Supercomputer Center uses Digital Equipment Corporation's (DEC) VAX and PDP-11 minicomputers to manage these tasks.

Input is the data or information that a user enters into the supercomputer to solve a calculation or problem. Programs that control the communications within the supercomputer use *protocols*, or specific standards that must be met, to access the computer. For example, problems from remote users of the SDSC supercomputer are managed by a protocol known as Network Service Protocol (NSP). The Department of Defense's Transmission Control Protocol/Internet Protocol (TCP/IP), which is part of the National Science Foundation's standard protocol throughout the country, has been added to the SDSC supercomputer for those scientists who need to use it.

Output are the results of running a problem or set of calculations through the supercomputer. Output can be sent back to the user's location where it can be viewed on a computer screen or printed out on the user's own equipment. Sometimes, output is printed at the SDSC, which can handle graphics as well as text.

SDSC also provides users with the means to visualize their output results. The San Diego center has a visualization laboratory (VisLab) with more than a dozen graphics workstations, hard-copy output devices, and applications software. The list of available equipment includes a choice of several graphics applications, a CD-ROM reader/scanner, and devices for image processing. The SDSC also provides services to help scientists create videotapes of their research results. Another specialized device can transfer computer images onto film, a capability that is especially useful for scientists doing research in areas such as aerodynamics, engineering, and biology. In addition, animation can be produced for movies and television.

Many researchers have used SDSCs Visualization Laboratory to "see" the results of their work by creating computer-generated simulations and graphics. Some of the studies that have been visualized in color at the SDSC include research on arterial blood flow, propagation of light in optical fibers, modeling of natural systems such as oceans and lakes, architectural design of buildings, design of ultrahigh-density disk storage, oscillations of pulsating stars, studies of air quality in cities such as Los Angeles, modeling of seismic response to show ground motion during earthquakes, and three-dimensional interpretations of ultrasound images of unborn babies during prenatal health care.

Communications:
Linking the Parts of the Supercomputer

In order for the many parts of the SDSC supercomputer to work together optimally, they must be properly linked. The main carrier of information is called a *hyperchannel*. Data transfers between the central processing unit and the DD49 disk drives used for storage of data occur at a speed of 100 million bytes per second. Channels connect the central processing unit with minicomputers that oversee the printer and other output data.

Some remotely located users of the SDSC supercomputer access the system using regular telephone lines. However, these telephone lines operate at very slow speeds compared to the supercomputer itself. Most *modems* operate at 1,200 or 2,400 bits per second, whereas the supercomputer moves data at 50 to 100 million bits per second. (A modem is a device that transforms digital data from a computer into analog form, which can be transmitted over communication lines such as telephone lines. The word *modem* is from the terms *mo*dulation-*dem*odulation, which describe the process. A modem can also receive data in an analog form and restore it to digital form so that information can flow both to and from a computer.) Hence, the data that must be transmitted to the supercomputer to solve or analyze a problem may take hours to input and the results hours to output to the user. Any interruption in the telephone lines can result in inaccurate data in the input or inaccurate results in the output.

The SDSC supercomputer can be accessed more efficiently using a network of dedicated communications lines known as SDSCNET that have been set up for this purpose. (A dedicated line is one used only for a single purpose.) This network of dedicated lines includes satellite communications for users who are at a distance, such as in Hawaii, as well as lines on land for users that are relatively near the SDSC. These dedicated lines operate at 56,000 bits per second, much faster than an ordinary modem and telephone line. A protocol that was developed at Lawrence Livermore National Laboratory and abbreviated MFENET directs the input and output from users to the SDSCNET.

The SDSC supercomputer is linked by electronic-mail networks, by NSF networks, and by a Department of Energy network to assist scientists and researchers to communicate with each other as well as to utilize the supercomputer itself.

This supercomputer visualization shows the components of smog. The pollutants are overlaid with Landsat imagery and a model grid. (Courtesy National Center for Supercomputing Applications)

Who Uses Supercomputers?

In its first year, 1986, the SDSC supercomputer was used mainly by scientists. The greatest usage was by physicists, biochemists, and chemists. Others included researchers in atmospheric sciences such as weather prediction and climate studies, materials science, astronomy, mathematics, earth science (including earthquake prediction), mechanics, and oceanography. Most of these users were affiliated with universities or other academic institutions.

The SDSC offers facilities such as an auditorium, conference rooms, and a large number of desktop computers for teaching people how to use the supercomputer most effectively. Seminars and workshops are held regularly to assist users. The SDSC has available many thousands of pages of information and documentation on how to use the supercomputer. The staff at SDSC also can be reached for help using the SDSCNET or by e-mail, regular mail, or telephone. The SDSC also publishes a newsletter and other information and makes its library of programs available for users.

The National Center for Supercomputing Applications located at the University of Illinois, Champaign/Urbana is another example of a supercomputing center. In contrast to the SDSC, the NCSA has four production supercomputers. One is a Connection Machine Model 5 (CM-5) with 512 nodes and 16 gigabytes of memory. Another is a Connection Machine Model 2 (CM-2) with 32,000 nodes, 1 gigabyte of memory, and 64-bit floating point hardware. In addition the NCSA has a CONVEX C3880 (C3) with eight processors, and 4 gigabytes of memory and a CRAY Y-MP4/464 with four processors and 64 million words of main memory.

One area that puts NCSA's sophisticated equipment to good use is its visualization program, which incorporates *virtual reality* (VR) to surround the user with an artificial environment that accurately simulates reality. Scientists can use a head-mounted display, a glove that allows the user to interact with the VR environment, and other hardware to experiment with problems such as

A training class is held at the Renaissance Educational Laboratory located at the National Center for Supercomputing Applications. (Courtesy National Center for Supercomputing Applications)

those in manufacturing, pharmaceutical design, and new ideas in education.

Like the other supercomputer centers, NCSA is continually updating its capabilities. An addition to the NCSA VR Laboratory is called CAVE. It is a collaboration between NCSA and the University of Illinois at Chicago's Electronic Visualization Laboratory. In CAVE, a VR environment is projected onto multiple walls of a room. The space is large enough for several people to experiment in the VR environment at one time.

As with other supercomputer centers, NCSA promotes the teaching of supercomputing visualization skills. At the Renaissance Experimental Laboratory (REL), located at University of Illinois, U/C's Beckman Institute, laboratory workstations are open to university faculty members who teach computer graphics in their courses. Courses have been available in subjects such as biophysics, computer science, mathematics, chemistry, and in art and design.

6

Supercomputers in Weather, Climate, and Agricultural Research

Of the many important ways in which supercomputers can be used, one of the most valuable is for basic scientific research. Researchers who work at the leading edge of new knowledge in many of the disciplines of science need the speed and power of supercomputers. From astronomy to physics to mathematics to the human genome project to weather prediction and more, researchers agree that today's fastest computers are still too slow. They seek ever greater computing power to find answers to their most complex problems.

Using Mathematics to Predict the Weather

One of the users of supercomputing power is the National Center for Atmospheric Research (NCAR) in Boulder, Colorado. It was founded in 1960 and is managed by an affiliated group of 14 universities known as the University Corporation for Atmospheric Research.

For most people, the only thing they want to know about the weather is: Will it rain in my location this afternoon, or what is the forecast for the weekend? However, the prediction of severe storms, hurricanes, droughts, or tornadoes can be far more important in saving crops and lives.

The branch of mathematics known as calculus deals with rates of change—the way one quantity varies in relation to other quantities such as location or time. Supercomputers allow scientists to use the mathematical equations of calculus to represent the dynamic, constantly changing, natural physical world and the laws that govern it. Rather than simply providing researchers with long lists of calculations, supercomputers also allow them to create visual representations of the physical world. Often these visual representations lead to important new insights that might not have been observed by looking at the numerical solutions alone.

Scientists have devised equations that can define and predict weather on a large scale; and parallel processing is well suited to handle the data used for weather forecasting. In weather studies, data is collected from points located on a three-dimensional grid that includes locations at the surface of the Earth and at a specified altitude in the atmosphere. A general circulation model uses data from three dimensions to simulate the way weather varies with latitude, longitude, and altitude. The data collected may include, not only temperature but also humidity, wind speed, wind direction, soil moisture, and other information.

For example, points in a grid at ground level may be 75 to 100 miles apart, and points in the atmosphere may be up to 2 miles in

Above: This is a computer simulation of one phase in the development of a tornadic storm. The three-dimensional surface shown encloses most of the region of rain within the storm. Below: This grid of the Earth showing North and South America is part of a computer simulation of the global effects of increased greenhouse gases on climate. (Both photographs courtesy: National Center for Supercomputing Applications)

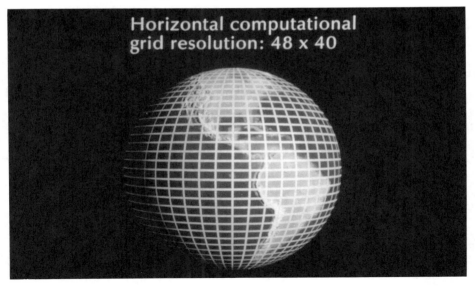

altitude above the Earth's surface. Problems arise predicting the weather because information collected from points many miles apart do not account adequately for local weather patterns that lie within each section of the grid. The closer the data points are to each other on the grid, the greater the accuracy of the weather prediction.

To get an idea of the need for greater computational power, a scientist named J. Smagorinsky found that a computer working at a speed of 5 million instructions per second and using a three-dimensional weather model with ground level data points 124 miles apart and with additional points 1.86 miles in the atmosphere required 2.4 hours of computation time to predict the weather 24 hours in the future. If the data points were at a closer range to each other, say at a distance of 31 miles apart on the ground and 0.47 miles in the atmosphere, the computer would take more than 153 hours to produce a prediction. That would be more than 129 hours after the weather had occurred!

Another aspect of weather prediction that makes greater computational power necessary is the problem of multiple-length scales (a common problem for many fields of scientific research). For example, the jet stream that flows across the United States and that greatly affects the weather is about 3,000 miles long and 200 miles wide. Individual large storm systems may be several hundred miles in diameter. But the currents of wind in a local thunderstorm may be very different within a distance of only 50 or 100 feet. Yet, the localized wind currents in the thunderstorm will interact with and affect the larger weather pattern.

Weather events on a small scale, such as squall lines, tornadoes, and wind shear are called mesoscale events. Meteorologists say that accurate weather forecasting must include data from both large-scale and small scale events because they do interact. With current computational power, the weather phenomena that occur within an individual grid are represented collectively. This means, for example, that an average temperature is used to represent the entire range of temperatures within a single section of the grid.

Other problems predicting weather result from the presence of phenomena such as cloud cover. Clouds reflect sunlight back into space, tending to cool the surface of the Earth. On the other hand, cloud cover traps heat that has been absorbed by the Earth near the ground's surface. Snow also makes temperature predictions difficult. When snow accumulates on the ground, it reflects sunlight rather than absorbing it like the dark, bare earth, and the result is that temperatures tend to be cooler where there is snow cover.

Long-range forecasting of the weather is important to agricultural workers and farmers, transportation workers, and electrical power companies. Farmers use such forecasts to plan when to plant, fertilize, treat with pesticides, and harvest their crops. Severe weather conditions may delay or reroute airline flights. Power companies can better determine times of peak demand for electricity for air-conditioning and other needs if temperature forecasts are known in advance.

The European Center for Medium-range Weather Forecasts (ECMWF) has a model that resolves the atmosphere into waves rather than horizontal grid points. Each latitude is surrounded by 106 waves, which is equivalent to a grid with points 1.1 degrees apart. For the vertical direction, the ECMWF divides the atmosphere into 19 levels.

The ECMWF installed a CRAY Y-MP with eight parallel processors that can sustain speeds of more than 1 gigaflop to handle the huge volume of data from the many levels and latitudes. It has made possible six-day weather forecasts that are now as reliable as those it made in the late 1970s for two or three days.

Global Climate Studies

Another way in which supercomputers are being used is to study global climate. Some scientists are researching the history of the Earth's climate. Many ancient records exist that give clues to the climate thousands of years ago. For example, bristle-cone pine trees live to be thousands of years old and, for this reason, the annual rings of these trees provide a record of climate changes. In China farmers recorded the dates of beginning of planting of crops, harvesting of crops, and first frost over a period of hundreds of years. These records were made available to scientists at NCAR.

The community climate model (CCM) is one of several computer models that have been developed to study the Earth's climate. It is used by about 40 universities doing climate research in the United States. Ongoing work using the CCM includes studies of the increase in size of the Sahara, ocean-temperature abnormalities such as El Niño (a periodic warming of the equatorial Pacific Ocean), and effects of changes in ocean temperatures near the Equator on rainfall in Brazil and other countries as far away as Zimbabwe.

How reliable are the supercomputer models for climate? One way to verify their accuracy is to see if the models can simulate current known climate conditions. Second, individual grids can be checked to see if the average data used in the model corresponds to the actual weather conditions within the grid. In addition, a model can be verified by seeing if it can reproduce paleoclimatic (ancient climate) conditions.

In a study done at the University of Wisconsin at Madison, John E. Kutzbach and his collaborators sought to explain a warm period that took place on Earth between 9,000 and 5,000 years ago. Fossil evidence suggests that the summer temperatures in the Northern Hemisphere were several degrees higher than they are now and that the monsoons in Asia and Africa were more severe then.

Kutzbach's simulation showed that the difference in temperatures could be due to two changes in the Earth's orbit. These changes were that the Earth had a slightly greater tilt on its axis and that the closest approach to the sun was made in June rather than in January as it does now. The effect of the change in tilt was that the northern continents received about 5 percent more heat from the sun in the summer and 5 percent less in the winter than today. Because the temperature differences between the ocean and the land were greater during that period, the patterns of the wind were altered and caused greater rainfall during the monsoon season.

In another paleoclimatic study, Stephen H. Schneider and Starley L. Thompson researched the causes of the sudden climate changes that occurred about 11,000 years ago as the Earth was emerging from the last Ice Age. Just as plants and animals were beginning to be able to survive and repopulate the more northern latitudes in western Europe, the temperature plummeted once again with the cooling effects greatest over the North Atlantic Ocean. This cold climatic period is known as the Younger Dryas and lasted for about 1,000 years.

Several paleoclimatologists think that the Younger Dryas was due to the breakup of ice sheets near the end of the Ice Age in Europe and North America. The melting of these sheets produced an enormous influx of fresh water into the ocean, and since fresh water freezes more readily than salt water, a vast cover of winter ice may have formed on the ocean, diverting the normal flow of the Gulf Stream into the North Atlantic. The warm waters of the Gulf Stream that usually moderate cold winter temperatures in northwestern Europe were blocked.

Studies at NCAR of ancient climate have revealed that approximately 100 million years ago, during the Cretaceous period, when the dinosaurs dominated the world, temperatures were significantly warmer. The results of such studies have been difficult to interpret because the continents have drifted since that time and because different climate models have been used. But it appears that Antarctica was free of ice, that the North Pole was warm enough then for alligators to live there, and that tropical plants thrived at high altitudes. One important unanswered question is whether the amount of carbon dioxide during the Cretaceous period was higher than at later periods in the Earth's history.

Carbon Dioxide and the Greenhouse Effect

Scientists who study the climate have agreed that carbon dioxide in the atmosphere has increased over the last half century. There are several reasons cited for this. Deforestation in many regions of the Earth continues to progress at a rate far faster than the trees can be replenished. This is important because trees prevent excess amounts of carbon dioxide from entering the atmosphere and give off oxygen as a byproduct of photosynthesis, the process green plants use to make sugar. In addition, the human population of the Earth has been growing steadily larger, with a current head count of approximately 5 billion. People need cleared land on which to live and to grow crops. Also, more fossil fuels are being burned, especially in heavily industrialized countries, adding to the carbon dioxide content of the atmosphere.

Supercomputer models of climate show that a significant increase in carbon dioxide in the air would cause the upper levels of the Earth's atmosphere to hold onto heat causing a so-called *greenhouse effect*. This would produce a warmer climate worldwide.

Greenhouse warming occurs because sunlight can easily enter the Earth's atmosphere and warm the ground. But infrared radiation given off by the warmed surface of the Earth cannot escape from the atmosphere. There is a natural capturing of heat due to the atmospheric water vapor surrounding the surface of the Earth, and this accounts for about 80 percent of the greenhouse effect. In fact, without this natural greenhouse effect, scientists think that much of the Earth's surface would be frozen. What concerns researchers, however, is that there has been an increase in greenhouse gases, principally carbon dioxide (CO_2), that is blamed on the burning of fossil fuels such as coal and oil as well as on other human activities.

In research done using a three-dimensional climate model, Eric J. Barron, who is now at Pennsylvania State University, and Warren M. Washington of NCAR tested the idea that ocean currents

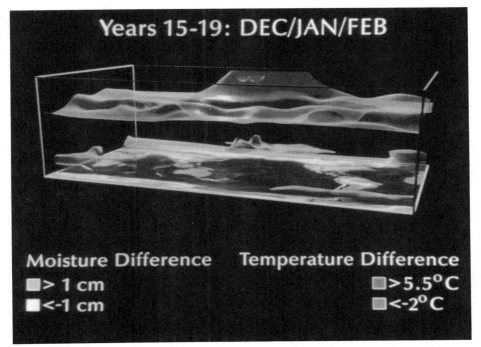

Years 15-19: DEC/JAN/FEB

Moisture Difference
■ > 1 cm
■ < -1 cm

Temperature Difference
■ > 5.5°C
■ < -2°C

This computer simulation of the global climatic effects of increased greenhouse gases shows the atmosphere in three dimensions, but with an exaggerated vertical scale. (Courtesy National Center for Supercomputing Applications)

were responsible for the warmer climate that prevailed during the Cretaceous period. Even when the temperature of the oceans was not allowed to drop below 20 degrees Celsius, including at the poles of the Earth, and the winds were strong enough to circulate the atmosphere, the model could not fully account for the warm climate. Some other factor helped to keep the climate warm. Schneider and his colleagues suspect that the other factor was elevated levels of carbon dioxide in the atmosphere.

In support of this suggestion, scientists note that there was a lot of tectonic plate motion during the mid-Cretaceous period. (Tectonic plates are huge, movable parts of the Earth's crust.) This would allow for the escape of carbon dioxide and other gases from the Earth's interior. The atmosphere during the Cretaceous may have had 5 to 10 times more carbon dioxide in it than is present today. What is significant about these studies is that the Cretaceous period may forecast a warmer future climate for the Earth if carbon dioxide continues to increase in the atmosphere.

Carbon dioxide was present in the atmosphere at a level of about 280 parts per million (ppm) 200 years ago, before the beginning of the Industrial Revolution. But since that time, the concentrations of carbon dioxide have increased by about 25 per-

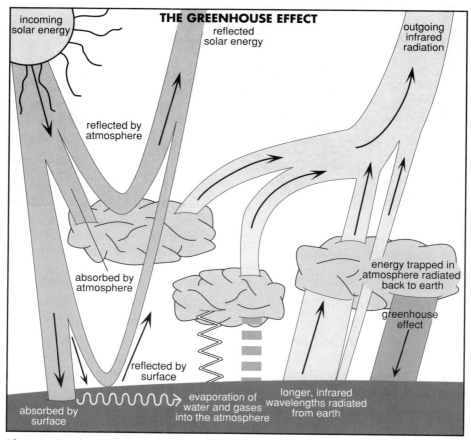

Figure 3 The greenhouse effect occurs when the atmosphere traps heat near the Earth's surface. Greenhouse gases, such as carbon dioxide, water vapor, and other gases, allow visible and near-infrared wavelengths of light from the sun to penetrate the Earth's atmosphere. The greenhouse gases also tend to absorb the longer, infrared wavelengths of light reflected by the Earth into the atmosphere and most of this energy then is radiated back to the Earth. For this reason, an increase in the concentration of greenhouse gases in the atmosphere tends to increase warming on the surface of the Earth.

cent to 355 ppm, as of 1992. If current increases continue, the amount of carbon dioxide in the atmosphere by 2050 will be double that of the 1800s prior to the Industrial Revolution.

Other Contributors to the Greenhouse Effect

The National Academy of Sciences has reported that the use of fossil fuels accounts for less than half of the recent increases in the greenhouse effect. Other contributors include a group of chemicals known as the chlorofluorocarbons (CFCs) that until recently were used as propellants in aerosol containers and as coolants in refrigerators, freezers, and air conditioners; nitrous oxide, which comes primarily from deforestation, the burning of vegetation, and nitrogen-based fertilizers; and methane, which comes from livestock and rice paddies.

The CFCs also are worrisome because they destroy the stratospheric ozone layer that serves to protect the Each from the Sun's excessive harmful ultraviolet radiation. When CFCs rise into the stratosphere, ultraviolet radiation from the Sun breaks down the bonds in the CFC molecule to release chlorine. The chlorine acts as a catalyst (a substance that increases the rate of a chemical reaction without being consumed) that destroys ozone. A single chlorine atom may break up thousands of ozone molecules. In addition to the hole in the ozone layer over the Antarctic, there also is a hole in the ozone layer over the Northern Hemisphere. Most countries in the world have now signed the Montreal Protocols that call for CFCs to be phased out of production by 1995.

Because CFCs are to be phased out of production, new coolants must be substituted for the old. One new group of chemicals are the hydrofluorocarbons (HFCs), which are formed by replacing chlorine in the CFC molecules with hydrogen. These compounds are much more reactive than the CFCs and for this reason will break down before reaching the ozone layer in the stratosphere. The Environmental Protection Agency has selected several of the HFCs for further study.

Researchers at DuPont have been using a supercomputer to evaluate the effects of using HFCs on the ozone layer and on global warming. David Dixon and his colleagues at DuPont can use a supercomputer to assess the properties of a new HFC within a few days using DuPont's CRAY Y-MP. For the National Institute of Standards and Technology to test and measure the properties of each new HFC by actual experimentation probably would take several months and cost thousands of dollars more to complete.

In addition to information about weather and climate that is available from earthbound sources, data from satellites and the space shuttle is now available to provide a new perspective to studies about climate and weather. With the advent of satellite and shuttle information, researchers have been reassessing how they view the planet Earth. More than ever, scientists from many different disciplines have adopted a global viewpoint and have realized that they must work together to achieve the best perspectives and models of the Earth's climate.

Project Sequoia 2000

A collaboration between the University of California and Digital Equipment Corporation (DEC) to study global climate is called Project Sequoia 2000. It combines the talents of earth scientists in fields such as meteorology, ecology, geochemistry, oceanography, bioclimatology, and hydrology with the talents of computer specialists to develop tools and methods to do global climate research. As in so many areas of research, there is an ever increasing amount of information that must be stored, analyzed, transferred, and visualized.

The objective of Project Sequoia 2000 is the creation of the infrastructure to handle global climate data from researchers working in each of the collaborating disciplines. The project is named after the long-lived sequoia trees that grow in the Sierra Nevada range in California. The year 2000 is added to indicate that the project will assess some of the most crucial issues of the next century. Global climate problems include ozone depletion, air and water pollution, deforestation, the greenhouse effect, loss of healthy vegetation, and decreasing potable (drinkable) water supplies.

To better visualize researchers' results, computer and graphics specialists are developing software that will allow scientists to "see" and manipulate information in *real time* (real time means that a process or event can be viewed as it is happening) using a network called *SequoiaNet*. Sets of data in the computer's system will be selected simply by pointing and clicking on the desired region of a world map and selecting the date and time when the data were recorded. Even the appropriate application needed by the researcher in his or her field will be stored so that the data can be interpreted using words and terms familiar to the particular researcher in his or her field.

Predicting the Effects of Nuclear War on Climate

In 1982 the first calculations were made of the effects on climate of a nuclear war. These studies were done by Paul J. Crutzen of the Max Planck Institute for Chemistry in Mainz, Germany and John W. Birks of the University of Colorado at Boulder. Their concern was that the thousands of devastating fires that would engulf areas of the Earth from nuclear explosions in a massive bombing would produce such heavy smoke in the atmosphere that sunlight would be significantly blocked. Another study known as the TTAPS model (taken from the initials of the surnames of its authors, Richard Turco, Owen Toon, Thomas Ackerman, James Pollack, and Carl Sagan) concluded that the Earth's temperatures on land would plummet an average of 20 to 40 degrees Celsius, causing a "nuclear winter."

The TTAPS model did not take into account the effects of winds, the possible moderating effects of the oceans, or the seasons of the year. Later studies were done by Curt Covey, Starley

Thompson, and Stephen Schneider at NCAR using a three-dimensional model. These studies showed that the moderating effects of the oceans would cut in half the drop in temperatures predicted by the authors of the TTAPS study.

Nevertheless, the effects on climate of a large-scale nuclear war would certainly be devastating. For instance, the NCAR study indicated that cooling could be very dramatic wherever dense smoke accumulated in the air even for a few days. Localized quick freezes could occur even in areas that would normally be warm during summer, such as the southern United States. The effects could wipe out food crops needed in the United States as well as foods normally exported to other countries.

More recent studies done at the Lawrence Livermore National Laboratory and the Los Alamos National Laboratory have agreed with the NCAR results that show that nuclear war would produce thick patches of clouds and would cause freezing temperatures on the ground beneath the cloud cover in the Northern Hemisphere.

Pest Control in Agriculture

The control of agricultural pests is an age old problem that continues to plague farmers. David Onstad, an associate professor of agricultural entomology at the University of Illinois, is using supercomputer models to study agricultural pests and to evaluate biological control methods. He uses the CRAY Y-MP and the Thinking Machines Inc. Connection Machine (model CM-2) at the National Center for Supercomputing Applications (NCSA) to analyze various agricultural control models.

There are many factors that help to control insect populations. These include disease, natural enemies, and unfavorable climate or habitat. Onstad says, "In order to evaluate the effectiveness of biological controls or predict their potential, it's important to understand the long term population dynamics of the pest and those of their natural enemies, including disease."

Onstad has used a computer model of the European corn borer to reveal ecological factors that influence the development of pests. With it he has helped predict how the corn borer population distributes itself as it infests a field. The model also can be used to evaluate biological controls for the corn borer and for other insect pests such as the gypsy moth.

Many farmers now use a method known as integrated pest management (IPM) to control insect pests. IPM requires growers to learn which pests affect their crops, their life cycles, and how to carefully monitor the pest populations on their crops. Whenever possible, nonchemical methods of pest control are used, including appropriate timing of planting and harvesting, crop rotation, and biological controls. When certain threshold numbers of pests are present despite the nonchemical control methods, pesticides may be applied.

In the summer of 1991, a severe outbreak in the United States of the European corn borer had farmers considering various control measures. Usually, two generations of corn borers are hatched each summer. The larvae, or wormlike stage of the insects, bore into corn stalks or the ears of corn, and when present in large enough numbers, they can destroy much of the crop. Nevertheless, many farmers are reluctant to apply pesticides and would prefer a non-chemical way to control the corn borers.

One answer may be to control the corn borer with a natural enemy. When the European corn borer accidentally arrived in the United States about 90 years ago, it had no natural enemies here. Since then, the U.S. Department of Agriculture has brought many natural enemies from Europe, and now Onstad has used his model to evaluate their effectiveness to control the corn borers.

A parasitic wasp, *Macrocentrus grandi,* was imported 40 years ago, but it has not been very effective in controlling corn borers. Some other parasitic insect enemies have not survived in the United States or have never multiplied adequately to be effective controls.

Onstad's model showed that the parasitic wasps have not been effective because of another disease-causing organism, *Nosema pyrausta*. This disease organism infects corn borers and weakens them, slows their rate of reproduction and in some individuals, kills them. However, in addition to infecting the corn borer, the disease also infects the parasitic wasps. Onstad's model also explained that when the corn borer population is low, the parasitic wasps cannot find enough larvae to survive and much of their population dies off. Hence, when corn borer populations are low, the parasitic wasps become an inefficient method of control.

In order to accurately visualize on a computer screen a model such as the one Onstad has devised for the European corn borer, many variables must be considered. As Onstad describes the task:

> . . . . I need to look at a hundred thousand pieces of information. If you want to have a hundred pixels represent each of those hundred thousand pieces of information then you need ten million pixels. [A *pixel* is one dot or element of an image that requires many dots or pixels to create the whole picture, such as the image on a TV screen.] So we need at least 10 times more pixels than we have now. Ten pixels per piece of information is not enough.

Already, Onstad is joining forces with other researchers to use his computer models and visualization techniques on other ecological problems. Dick Warner, director of the Center for Wildlife Ecology of the Illinois Natural History Survey, and Onstad will create a model of the changing habitat for Illinois wildlife and study its effects on the wildlife populations. In order to achieve an accurate representation of changes in the habitat and wildlife population, many factors must be studied including weather, loss of habitat, diseases, and pesticide contamination. Another University of Illinois professor, Brian Orland, will work with Onstad to study pests that infest forests in the western United States as well as how fires affect the growth of forests.

7
∇

SUPERCOMPUTERS AID HUMAN RESEARCH PROJECTS

*A*ll life on Earth carries within it information that is coded into its *genes*, the hereditary units that are passed from one generation of any living thing to the next. The coded information is located within molecules known as *deoxyribonucleic acid* (DNA) and ribonucleic acid (RNA). These two molecules are composed of long sequences of smaller molecular structures called *nucleotides*. Each nucleotide, in turn, consists of a sugar, a phosphate group, and a base.

DNA has four bases known as adenine (A), guanine (G), thymine (T), and cytosine (C), only one of which may be part of each nucleotide. In RNA, the base thymine is replaced by the base uracil (U). Different arrangements of the four bases, A, G, T, and C in DNA, serve as a genetic code that can produce different genetic traits and that carries the instructions on how to create a living creature or plant. In DNA, two strands of nucleotides wrap together into a helix shape; bases are paired in specific ways.

A sequence of three nucleotide bases along the DNA molecule codes for one *amino acid*. There are 20 amino acids that are the basic building blocks of all of the proteins found in living things. A gene is a sequence of nucleotide bases on a chromosome that determines the order of amino acids in a protein molecule. A human has 23 pairs of chromosomes, each of which contains thousands of genes. RNA molecules copy the DNA nucleotide base sequences for each gene and serve as messengers and templates to produce protein molecules. Different protein molecules have distinct shapes that enable them to perform specific functions. For example, different protein molecules can serve as antibodies (which fight infection), enzymes (which are biological catalysts that speed up or start chemical reactions), or parts of the structure of the cells of the animal or plant.

The image shows a computer simulation of a DNA molecule in three dimensions. (Courtesy Silicon Graphics and Anthony Nicholls, Barry Honig of Columbia University)

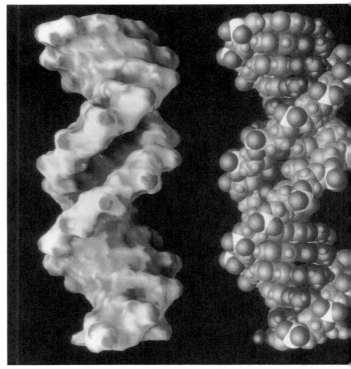

The Human Genome Project

The Human Genome Project is a grand-challenge project that seeks to map—that is, locate on a specific chromosome—all of the genes present in human beings. In countries all over the world, there are many scientists working on the Human Genome Project. One of them, Douglas W. Smith, is a professor of biology at the University of California, San Diego (UCSD). He and his assistants developed a program they call SEARCH.

For years, scientists have been gathering genetic information and storing it in large databases for future use. What SEARCH does is to compare a DNA sequence of unknown function to known protein sequences that have been accumulated in databases. What may at first seem like a straightforward problem of computation really is much more complex because genes may contain additions, deletions, or small changes that do not prevent them from functioning.

SEARCH was originally developed to use on sequential computers, but it can be used on parallel supercomputers such as the San Diego Supercomputer Center's Intel Paragon. Recently, a graduate student from UCSD, Josh Jorgenson, found that the Paragon would speed up research measurements significantly. It could compare a gene consisting of 4,000 bases to a large protein database in about 10 seconds.

The SEARCH program can help seek out and identify disease-related genes in human DNA. Of interest is that about 70 percent of a human being's genes are identical to those of a mouse. Estimates are that all human beings have identical genes to within one part in a thousand. Amazingly, all of our physical differences and about 3,000 genetically linked diseases are found within the relatively small differences in our genetic inheritance. Parallel supercomputers can compare sequences rapidly and will be important in solving problems related to human disease and to the whole scope of the Human Genome Project.

Dr. Francis Collins has become the head of the National Center for Human Genome Research (NCHGR) at the National

Institutes of Health (NIH). He was a candidate for his doctoral degree in physical chemistry at Yale University when he first took a course in biochemistry and encountered DNA and RNA. He says of his initial meeting with these molecules that carry the code of life, "I was completely blown away." Dr. Collins enrolled in medical school at the University of North Carolina and studied medical genetics. He has since pursued disease-causing genes and was one of the researchers who found the genes that cause cystic fibrosis and neurofibromatosis.

One of the biggest challenges of the Human Genome Project is managing all of the data being collected throughout the world. For the information to be useful, it must be accessible and researchers must be able to manipulate it. There are three primary databases and each one stores a different kind of genetic information. GenBank stores DNA sequences, Genome Data Base stores chromosome mapping information, and Protein Information Resource stores data on protein sequence and structure. Each of these databases has its own system for collecting and storing information. Scientists want to link the primary databases and to adopt a standard protocol to retrieve related data from all of the sources.

James Ostell is the chief of the information engineering branch at the National Center for Biotechnology Information (NCBI) at the National Institutes of Health. Ostell calls the method of storing and analyzing genetic and biological information "bioinformatics." Researchers want to have immediate access to all of the information related to the genes they are studying. They say that if they could learn what other researchers have discovered about similar genes, they might find clues to the function of a new genetic sequence they have uncovered.

What is needed is an integrated system of information, but scientists from all over the world have not agreed to the best way to accomplish this. It appears that one solution may be to have the most frequently used data centralized into a single large data bank and the less frequently used data affiliated into a worldwide federation of information that doesn't require all of the data to conform to a common format.

When the Human Genome Project was started at the beginning of this decade, its planners thought of it as a 15-year project. But in the December 1993/January 1994 issue of *New Scientist*, the first "map" of the human genome was already reported by Daniel Cohen and other scientists in Paris, France. The work was done at Genethon and its companion laboratory, the Centre d'Etude du Polymorphisme Humaine (CEPH) in Paris. At Genethon, robots prepare thousands of DNA samples and a dozen other machines test for DNA sequences.

The French map divides the DNA into smaller, manageable pieces. Each DNA fragment is like a book that needs much more research to learn the details of the story. The entire human genome contains about 3 billion paired nucleotides spread among 23 pairs of chromosomes; hence much work remains to be done. But this first physical map of all 24 (22 chromosomes plus the male and female chromosomes, Y and X, respectively) human chromosomes is ready far sooner than was expected and is an extraordinary achievement.

Supercomputers and the Human Heart

Engineers and scientists study the flow of fluids through pipes, engines, and complicated machinery. But mechanical devices can not compare to the complexity of a living animal or to the demands of the pumping human heart. Researchers David M. McQueen and Charles S. Peskin of the Courant Institute of Mathematical Sciences in New York have studied the flow of blood through the human heart in an effort to design better artificial heart valves. Their studies used supercomputers to simulate heart action and to analyze blood flow through the heart.

The human heart is a strong muscular pump that consists of four chambers: the right auricle, the right ventricle, the left auricle, and the left ventricle. The two auricles are relatively thin-walled when compared to the two more muscular ventricles. It is the thick-walled right ventricle that pumps blood to the lungs to pick

David M. McQueen and Charles S. Peskin of the Courant Institute of Mathematical Sciences in New York study the flow of blood through the human heart using supercomputers to simulate heart action and to analyze blood flow through the heart. (Courtesy New York University Archives)

up the oxygen molecules needed by all cells of the body. Then this oxygenated blood returns to the left auricle, passes through the mitral valve, and is pumped by the left ventricle throughout the rest of the body.

The mitral valve consists of two triangular-shaped flaps of tissue that open and close to regulate the flow of blood from the left auricle to the left ventricle. When disease ravages the heart valve, surgeons would prefer to replace the damaged valve with a donor valve from another human. However, a mitral valve is not always available when needed.

One of the difficult problems in designing artificial heart valves is that the blood, which is itself a living tissue, must be kept moving rapidly enough to prevent the formation of blood clots. Stagnant blood may clot and can produce great damage or even prove deadly if a clot breaks loose and circulates to a critical area such as the brain or to blood vessels that nourish the heart muscle itself. In addition, artificial heart valves must not interfere with the normal rhythm of the beating heart, which is regulated by electrical signals generated naturally within the heart muscle.

Two of the items that McQueen and Peskin studied were the velocities of the flow of blood through artificial heart valves and the curvature of the small leaflets of the valve that open and close during heartbeats. Using a supercomputer to simulate blood flow and the action of the beating heart, they analyzed how different heart valve designs affect the flow of blood through the heart. With their simulations and test results, the two researchers were able to identify the most efficient curvature for the leaflets of the valves and the best pivot point for each valve that they tested. They also found that in valves with curved leaflets, a constraint was needed to keep the valves functioning at their best levels to prevent blood clots.

8

$\overline{\vee}$

SUPERCOMPUTERS REACH FOR THE STARS

---

*I*n a book written by Heinz R. Pagels, *Perfect Symmetry*, published by Simon and Schuster in 1985, the author asks:

> These great islands of stars are arranged in a hierarchy consisting of galaxies, clusters of galaxies, and super clusters. Why does the universe arrange itself in this peculiar way? Why, for example, aren't the stars, or even the galaxies, uniformly distributed in space?

An example of a star-cluster simulation. (Courtesy National Center for Supercomputing Applications)

How Are Supercomputers Being Used to Study the Universe?

One of the big questions astronomers have wrestled with for centuries is how galaxies are formed. Two theories are in competition with each other. One is called the "bottom-up" theory. It states that the first structures in galaxies were small in size. These small protogalaxies (the prefix *proto* means "before or first in time") of dense, cold clouds of gas clustered together to form the superclusters we see today.

The second theory is known as the "top-down" theory. As the name suggests, this presents an opposite view of galaxy formation from the bottom-up theory. The top-down theory predicts that superclusters formed first and then later they fragmented into galaxies. A Russian scientist, Yakob B. Zel'dovich, theorized that superclusters in the early universe would eventually collapse, most probably into a flattened structure that he described as a pancake. His theory predicts that the collapse would produce fragmentation because of gravitational instability.

To explore this mystery, Wenbo Y. Anninos, a postdoctoral research associate at NCSA, used special astrophysical fluid-dynamics software named ZEUS-2D (2D to indicate two dimensions) to simulate the collapse and fragmentation of the pancakes Zel'dovich had predicted. To pursue her goal, Anninos incorporated information to describe the expansion of the universe as well as other data into the ZEUS-2D computer program that would create a more complete model for the primordial plasma material from which the galaxies have formed.

"The simulation had been done in one dimension before and demonstrated the collapse, but they could not observe fragmentation," says Anninos. Using ZEUS-2D, Anninos was able to see fragmentation. In addition, she made the new discovery that gravitational instability was accompanied by cooling instability to produce fragmentation.

In a visual galaxy simulation using ZEUS-2D, Anninos depicted gas density, gas temperature, gas pressure, and dark-matter density. She was able to show dense cold gas clouds, which are protogalaxies, formed from pancake fragmentation. Anninos's work has added to our knowledge of the top-down theory of galaxy formation predicted by Zel'dovich.

Another related area of research is in gas dynamics. Gas dynamics is the study of the behavior of gases when they are affected by pressure, gravity, radiation, magnetic fields, and other forces. To advance research in the field of gas dynamics, David Clarke, a postdoctoral research associate and fellow at NCSA, and Michael Norman, NCSA research scientist and University of Illinois U/C professor of astronomy, developed ZEUS-3D to study gas dynamics in three dimensions. These three-dimensional simulations can take more than 100 hours to compute on a CRAY-2 supercomputer and output can be more than 10 gigabytes of data.

"For astrophysicists, generating models in 3D represents more than just a quantitative improvement over doing the problems in 2D," says Clarke. "Three-dimensional modeling is *qualitatively* different from anything that has ever been attempted before—it enables us to generate 'numerical observations' of astrophysical systems impossible to observe otherwise. With a fully 3D simulation, one can perform the line-of-sight integrations necessary to determine how a telescope might observe an astrophysical system."

Wenbo Anninos is using ZEUS-3D to continue her study of galaxy formation. She is testing conditions that allow for either the bottom-up or the top-down theories, concentrating on areas where gravitational and cooling instability are important. Anninos says, "Our ultimate goal will be to use the ZEUS-3D simulation to distinguish which theory—bottom-up or top-down—is correct." Norman adds, "The problem is one that to do it right will require teraflop computers and a large computer science team."

Black Holes and Gravitational Waves

Another group of researchers at NCSA is studying the signatures of gravitational waves associated with *black holes* in space. Black holes are believed to be stars that have collapsed into a dense mass with a gravitational force so powerful that even light cannot escape. The signature of a gravitational wave is its unique characteristics that tells it apart from other gravitational waves, similar to how a fingerprint can identify an individual human being.

The U.S. government has funded construction of two laser interferometric gravitational wave observatories (LIGOs). With the LIGOs, scientists will try for the first time to measure the gravitational waves predicted by Albert Einstein in his general theory of relativity. In this theory, Einstein defines *gravity* as variations in the curvature of spacetime and predicts that cataclysmic events such as the collision between black holes or the exploding of a supernova send gravitational waves through the universe. The gravitational waves should be detectable as they pass near the Earth. With the

LIGOs researchers may be able to prove whether or not Einstein's theory of gravitation is correct.

NCSA scientist Ed Seidel is using supercomputer power to create a catalog of gravitational wave signatures that will help other researchers identify the sources of gravitational waves that they detect in the course of their own work. "Most systems have a normal mode frequency, just like a bell," says Seidel. "If you hit a bell, it rings with a certain frequency [which we hear as a particular pitch or musical tone]. Different sized bells have different frequencies [small bells have a higher pitch or musical tone than large bells]. Black holes also have special frequencies—only the wave being propagated is a gravitational wave."

Scientists have been able to understand the wave form for two black-hole systems during the time when they are far apart and after they have collided. However, Seidel says that no way has been devised to show what happens as two black holes come near each other and as they interact. Solving Einstein's equations is one of the grand-challenge problems of scientific research. The scope of the work includes collaborators at the University of Texas, the University of North Carolina, Cornell University, the University of Pittsburgh, and Northwestern University, as well as others. Seidel says, "Just think what would happen once we develop the technology to solve the general Einstein equations. The knowledge about these equations could just explode— . . ."

9

SUPERCOMPUTERS
MODEL
NEW MATERIALS

*D*uring the Middle Ages, alchemists tried to transform base metals such as lead into gold. Although they never succeeded in their quest, modern-day scientists are creating new materials using supercomputers. Instead of being limited to the materials provided by nature, researchers are using supercomputing power to design new materials with characteristics that are tailored to particular needs.

Supercomputers Are Used to Study Materials with New Properties

One of the pioneers of materials research is Arthur J. Freeman, Morrison professor of physics at Northwestern University and a user of NCSA's CRAY supercomputers. In 1980 Professor Freeman, postdoctoral associates Henry Krakauer and Erich Wimmer, and graduate student Michael Weinert developed a technique called the full potential linearized plane wave (FLAPW) method. It is used to calculate the electronic structure and properties of materials.

With FLAPW, Professor Freeman and his colleagues were able to predict that the level of magnetism of some common magnetic materials was much greater at the surface of the material than within the bulk of the material. They found, for example, that the level of magnetism of surface layer atoms in the metal iron was approximately 40 percent higher in the surface layer of iron atoms than in the inner bulk atoms. Experiments at the University of California at Berkeley proved their prediction to be correct.

In other related discoveries, Freeman and his associates found that magnetism is enhanced even more when a single atomic layer (monolayer) of certain materials is formed. For instance, when a single layer of chromium is deposited on gold, the level of magnetism

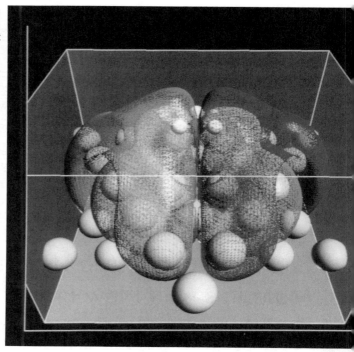

The image shows a three-dimensional computer simulation of an atom of gold. (Courtesy National Center for Supercomputing Applications)

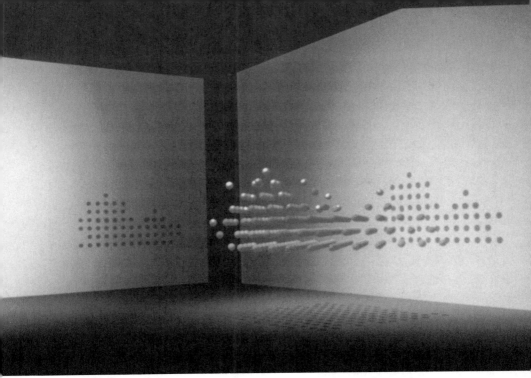

The dynamics of hydrogen collision on a rough nickel surface. The computer simulation shows how low-energy ions interact with solid surfaces. These interactions are being studied because they are at the heart of semiconductor processing and manufacture and research in fusion energy. (Courtesy National Center for Supercomputing Applications)

is up to six times greater than that present in bulk atoms within a piece of chromium. Also new is the finding that some normally nonmagnetic materials can become magnetic when they are deposited in a single layer of atoms onto another base material. For example, ordinarily, vanadium is not magnetic, but if a single layer of the element is deposited onto a base of silver, it becomes magnetic.

In speaking of supercomputers, Professor Freeman says, "These beautiful machines represent a new frontier which is driving the field of artificial materials." In addition to the magnetic properties of materials, supercomputers are being used to explore the electrical properties of monolayers and ultrathin films. These areas of research are of great importance to the continued development of semiconductors and microchips.

Superconductors

An area of intense research that is being pursued worldwide at breakneck speed is high-temperature superconductors. Scientists foresee many uses for superconducting materials.

In 1911, Dutch scientist Heike Kamerlingh Onnes was studying the effects of very cold temperatures on metals. While working with the metal mercury, he noticed that when the metal was cooled to the extremely low temperature of liquid helium, it allows electricity to flow through it without resistance. Onnes and other researchers experimented with other metals and learned that many of them also were superconductors when cooled in liquid helium. Onnes's discovery seemed of no practical importance because of the high expense of maintaining extremely cold temperatures with liquid helium.

Heike Kamerlingh Onnes, shown here in his laboratory, discovered the phenomenon of superconductivity in the metal mercury in 1911. (Photo from Rijksmuseum voor de Goschiedenis der Natuurwetenschappen te Leiden, courtesy Niels Bohr Library, American Institute of Physics)

Though additional work was done by scientists to seek a superconductor that would operate at higher temperatures, no significant improvement occurred until 1986. Two researchers who worked for IBM in Zurich, Switzerland, K. Alexander Müller and J. George Bednorz, decided to try working with some new kinds of ceramic materials. Although ceramics usually act as insulators, some of them behave somewhat like metals and these are called *perovskites.*

The two researchers spent three years testing hundreds of different perovskite samples. At last, in 1986, they hit upon a

---

material that became superconducting at the temperature of 30°K. *K* stands for Kelvin, a temperature scale devised by a British scientist, William Thomson, Lord Kelvin. Lord Kelvin was intrigued by just how cold things could get and reasoned that if the temperature became low enough, the molecules in matter would stop moving and would contain no energy. This temperature is called *absolute zero* and is equivalent to −273.15 degrees Celsius or 273.15 degrees below the freezing point of water.

Once Müller and Bednorz's discovery became known, a worldwide race began to try to find materials that would act as superconductors at higher and higher temperatures. The first step was to find a superconducting material that would operate at 77°K. This temperature was considered to be a "magic" threshold because at 77°K liquid nitrogen, which is much less costly than liquid helium, could be substituted for liquid helium as the coolant.

In January 1987 Dr. Paul Chu and his colleague, Dr. Maw-Kuen Wu, succeeded in reaching beyond the "magic" threshold to achieve superconductivity at a temperature above 90°K. The superconducting material they used was an oxide of the metals yttrium, barium, and copper described by the chemical formula $Y_{(1)}Ba_2Cu_3O_7$. This compound has become known as the 1-2-3 superconductor after its first three subscript numbers.

Researchers are seeking the fundamental reasons for the extraordinary behavior of super-

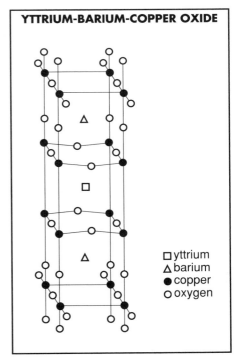

YTTRIUM-BARIUM-COPPER OXIDE

□ yttrium
△ barium
● copper
○ oxygen

Figure 4 This drawing shows the lattice structure of the high-temperature superconducting ceramic material known as yttrium-barium-copper oxide.

conductors. In 1957, three scientists, John Bardeen, Leon N. Cooper, and J. Robert Schrieffer, published a theory, the BCS theory (after the initials of the researchers), to try to explain superconductivity. It states that during superconductivity, electrons within the lattice structure of the superconducting material pair up as they flow through the material. Unlike ordinary conductors in which electrons travel individually through the material and collide with other atoms, the paired electrons in a superconducting material, called Cooper pairs, move in a nearly collision-free path as they travel through the superconducting material.

The BCS theory explains superconductivity in low-temperature materials such as mercury and lead. However, after Müller and Bednorz's discovery of ceramic materials that are high-temperature superconductors, a new theory was needed to adequately explain their behavior.

TEMPERATURE SCALES

British scientist William Thomson, Lord Kelvin, was intrigued by how cold substances could get. Absolute zero is the temperature at which the molecules in matter stop moving and contain no heat or energy. This chart compares some temperatures on the Celsius, Fahrenheit, and Kelvin scales. To devise the Kelvin scale, Thomson measured all temperatures from absolute zero upward in Celsius degrees. Absolute zero on the Kelvin scale is the same as 273.15 Celsius degrees below the freezing point of water.

	Celsius Degrees	Fahrenheit Degrees	Kelvin Scale
Water freezes	0	32	273.15
Water boils	100	212	373.15
Room temperature	20	68	293
Body temperature	37	98.6	310
Absolute zero	–273.15	–459.67	0

The intense interest in high-temperature superconductivity was demonstrated at a special meeting of the American Physical Society in New York City in January 1987. The occasion became known as the "Woodstock of Physics" when 4,000 people showed up and tried to crowd into a hall that was meant to hold only 2,000 people. There was standing room only to hear the lastest advances in high-temperature superconducting materials research!

By 1988, a group of scientists at the University of Arkansas discovered a thallium-barium-calcium-copper-oxygen compound ($Tl_2Ba_2Ca_2Cu_3O_{10}$) that would superconduct at 125°K. The global quest continues. Ultimately, the goal is to find a substance that will superconduct at room temperature, or approximately 300° K. At this temperature, no special coolants would be needed and superconductivity could be used for many everyday applications including the creation of superfast supercomputers.

Dr. David Pines has studied superconductivity for 40 years and continues to be fascinated by the behavior of these materials. He considers three questions to be of greatest importance in the study of superconductivity: What is the nature of the material's normal state? What is the character of the superconducting state? What is the physical origin of superconductivity?

Pines studied experiments done by physicist Charles Slichter and his team of researchers at the University of Illinois, Urbana, Champaign. Pines says, "These show that the magnetic behavior of the new superconductors is quite bizarre." Pines decided that a key role must be the magnetic interaction between the electrons in these systems. Pines continues, "The basic cause of the magnetic interaction is associated with the fact that electrons have a spin [either up or down] and therefore are capable of interacting magnetically through their spins. In . . . high-temperature superconductors, this magnetic interaction between the electrons can be very strong, changing their normal state of behavior and causing the superconducting transition."

To further study the behavior of high-temperature superconductors, Dr. Pines has said it is very important to start out with the right model. Of the long and complicated calculations required,

Pines explains, "You can only do this in a reasonable period of time with a supercomputer."

Even with a supercomputer, completing the calculations to the degree of accuracy needed requires the most up-to-date techniques. Philippe Monthoux, a postdoctoral physicist at the Institute for Theoretical Physics, University of California at Santa Barbara, has studied superconductivity and says that modeling the frequencies within a high-temperature superconductor uses the outer limits of the CRAY supercomputer system's memory and that his calculations took about 150 hours of CRAY time.

The experiments Drs. Pines and Monthoux did using the superconducting material yttrium-barium-copper-oxide (which superconducts at 90°K), described the material as a quite new state of matter. However, several separate groups of researchers have experimentally confirmed the findings of the Monthoux/Pines theory, and Monthoux is doing more studies on superconductivity using the Thinking Machines' CM-5 supercomputer at NCSA.

If high-temperature superconductors can be found and applied for practical commercial purposes, they may make economically feasible magnetically levitated trains, improvements in the generation of electrical power, new electronic devices, and even supercomputers that operate at much faster speeds than those available today.

Supercomputers Help in the Study of "Buckyballs"

In 1985 a new molecule composed of 60 carbon atoms was discovered. It includes 20 hexagons and 12 pentagons that are arranged in a shape like a soccer ball or a geodesic dome. The molecule is named *buckminsterfullerene* after Buckminster Fuller, inventor of the geodesic dome. Researchers have given the molecule the nickname "buckyball." Because carbon is an element that has been studied

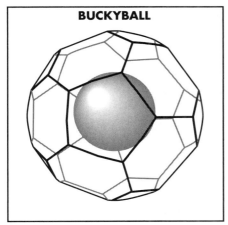

BUCKYBALL

Figure 5 This drawing of a molecule of buckminsterfullerene, or "buckyball," shows a neon atom trapped inside of its structure. This is the first stable neon compound ever discovered.

for many years, it is startling to learn that the buckyball was only recently discovered.

Buckyballs have a hollow form that may make them useful in certain chemical reactions. Researchers at Yale University have located an opening or "window" in the buckyball molecule. They were able to introduce an atom of neon through the opening to form the first known stable compound of neon. The Yale chemists also were able to do the same thing with helium, and until these feats were accomplished, no one thought that stable compounds of neon or helium could exist.

These new compounds were formed by heating buckyballs in the presence of either neon or helium to at least 600°C. The increased temperature apparently breaks a bond that links the carbon atoms in the buckyball, allowing a neon or helium atom to enter into the hollow center of the buckyball. Then, as the temperature falls, the "window" closes with the atom of gas inside. The buckyball is like a cage with the neon or helium atom trapped inside.

Buckyballs also can act as semiconductors, or, if tiny quantities of impurities are added, they become superconductors that have operated at temperatures as high as 45°K.

The spherical molecule also may be useful as a lubricant. It has been suggested that buckminsterfullerene could be used as a coating on ships to reduce friction as they slice through the ocean.

In paint form, buckyballs could reduce drag and turbulence in pumps, pipes, and bearings.

By studying buckyballs with supercomputers, Jerry Bernholc and coworkers at North Carolina State University learned that buckyballs had some unusual characteristics. For example, when buckyballs are heated, the heat causes each buckyball to spin billions of times per second, and the molecules stay intact up to temperatures of 2000°K.

Looking for What Everything Is Made of

Supercomputers can be used to simulate the behavior of the atomic and subatomic particles of matter that make up the universe. Scientists divide the world of subatomic particles into two groups. One group is called *bosons*, and an example of a boson is the basic unit of light called the photon. The other group is called *fermions*, and examples of the members of this group are the electrons, protons, and neutrons that make up individual atoms.

Researchers are trying to determine the fundamental particles that make up all matter in the universe by studying subatomic particles. In the 1960s, the fundamental particles of the atom were thought to be protons and neutrons. But scientist Murray Gell-Mann thought that protons and neutrons were themselves made up of still smaller particles. He called these smaller particles *quarks*, after a nonsense syllable he had read in a passage from James Joyce's *Finnegan's Wake*.

Physicists think of an electron as having no internal structure and consisting of a single infinitesimally tiny point of mass and electric charge. Researchers working with particle accelerators have found that protons and neutrons have a measurable diameter of approximately one-millionth of a nanometer. Protons and neutrons are made of particles called quarks that are thought to be true elementary particles.

∇

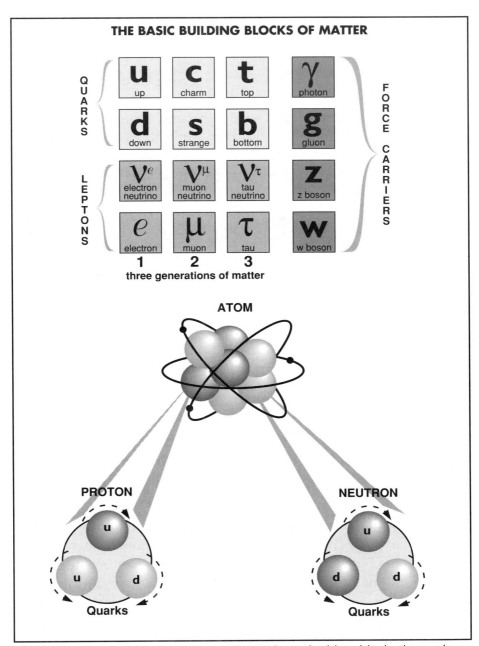

Figure 6 These drawings represent the 16 basic building blocks that make up all matter and that control how matter interacts. Physicists have used supercomputers to collect and analyze research data to determine what all matter is made of and to predict how it will behave.

A new law of nature known as quantum chromodynamics (QCD) developed during the 1970s. It explains how quarks interact and their relationship to another kind of particle called a *gluon*. Gluons carry what physicists call the strong force; the attraction that binds quarks together.

Except for quarks, electrically charged elementary particles have their charge in whole-number multiples of the electron's charge (which is -1). Quarks, on the other hand, have a fractional electric charge of $+\frac{2}{3}$, $-\frac{1}{3}$, or $+\frac{1}{3}$, and there are three quarks in each proton or neutron.

In addition to their fractional electric charge, quarks have another unusual characteristic, which physicists call their "color." A quark's color (which also is a nonsense term that has nothing to do with actual color) can be red, green, or blue and effects how they combine. To add further to this stranger-than-fiction world, quarks are said to come in six "flavors," or types: up, down, strange, charm, bottom, and top.

Unlike the power of electric charge, which diminishes as particles get further away from each other, quarks and gluons interact more strongly when the distance between them increases within a proton. For this reason, as a quark moves away from the other quarks within a proton (or neutron), the other two quarks pull on it with a force so strong that the proton is kept whole. Physicists call this behavior *quark confinement*.

Recently at the Fermi Laboratory in Batavia, Illinois as reported in the *Boston Sunday Globe* and other newspapers on March 5, 1995, physicists have found the top quark, which they believe is the last one of the fundamental building blocks of all the matter in the universe. They believe that top quarks may have existed in the first billionth of a second following the creation of the universe and that they have recreated top quarks by simulating that instant in time in the particle accelerator at the Fermi Lab. Energy Secretary Hazel O'Leary acclaimed the discovery as a "major contribution to human understanding of the fundamentals of the universe."

Another individual who has done work on subatomic particles is physicist Julius Kuti. He and some of his coworkers at the

University of California at San Diego and at Santa Barbara have used hundreds of hours annually on a Cyber 205 computer and an ST-100 array processor located in Santa Barbara, California.

Professor Kuti has used supercomputers to try to determine at what temperature the strong force holding quarks together can be overcome. In other words, at what point do gluons become unglued? He has said that supercomputers have "demonstrated rather convincingly" that quarks can escape the strong force exerted by gluons at about 200 million electron volts or a temperature of many trillions of degrees. There are probably a few hundred researchers studying QCD, and a number of them have used supercomputers to analyze their work.

Physicists have stated that the three pairs of quarks they have discovered have determined that our universe is dominated by matter and not by its absence. Frank Close, physicist at Britain's Rutherford and Appleton Laboratory, has said, "We are all made of atoms that have positively charged nuclei surrounded by negatively charged electrons, a type of matter that abounds wherever we look in the universe. *Antimatter* (atoms with negatively charged nuclei and positively charged electrons) is noticeably absent. We can only account for this state of affairs if there are three pairs of quarks. The mathematics is obstruse, but convincing."

Of the three pairs of quarks, the bottom and top quarks play the greatest part in determining the prevalence of matter.

The discovery of the top quark is important because physicists now have shown that their theory or standard model of the universe is complete and correct. Few physicists think that all has been discovered, however. They believe that the Large Hadron Collider, which European Cern wishes to construct by early in the next century, will be capable of recreating the explosive energies necessary to simulate the first moments of the big bang at the birth of the universe billions of years ago. In those fleeting moments of the simulation, the LHC should spew out top and bottom quarks and perhaps many new, unexpected particles.

10
∇
SUPERCOMPUTERS IN INDUSTRY AND DESIGN

Supercomputers Are Designing High-performance Aircraft

Modern aircraft manufacturers are in a very competitive business. Airplanes that are built today will remain in service for 20 years or more, so designing them to achieve the greatest efficiency, ease of maintenance, and lowest cost to purchase and to operate are important to each manufacturer.

A typical sequence in the development of aircraft is to use reduced scale models of aircraft in wind tunnels to simulate flight conditions to test designs. Building wind tunnels and doing experimentation with models is a costly and time-consuming process. Within the wind tunnel, the scale-model airplane is tested with

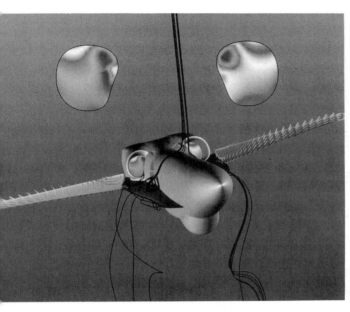

This model of an F18 airplane was created on a Silicon Graphics system by Mary Vickerman of NASA at the Lewis Research Center using a Fast Analysis Software Toolkit (FAST). (Courtesy Silicon Graphics)

many demands on its performance. Manufacturers need to know the maximum limits of gravitational forces and other stresses that it can withstand, how fast it can climb, how well it can turn, and whether or not the engine can avoid stalling.

If a model is successful, a prototype of the aircraft is built to test the design on a working, full-scale model of the airplane. Test pilots then take on the dangerous task of flying the aircraft to uncover any unforeseen problems with the design. For example, the test pilot may find that the engine does not perform as well as expected or that a surface on the wing of the plane flutters because it is under greater stress than anticipated.

With supercomputers, new ways to simulate the testing of aircraft are possible. As with other scientific work involving the flow of air or liquids, *fluid dynamics* is the branch of physics needed to study the complex flow of air around an airplane fuselage, wing, or jet engine.

In 1823 Claude Louis M. H. Navier published equations that mathematically described the flow of fluids such as air and water. In 1840 Sir George C. Stokes generalized the equations, but they still were too complex to use except with very simple problems. In the 1880s, another physicist, Osburne Reynolds, used the speed, density, and viscosity of the flow of materials to work out a formula to determine the onset of turbulence.

Nearly a century after Reynolds's work, the solutions to equations describing complex fluid dynamics and turbulence have not been possible. Scientists have had to use a simplified set of equations called the Reynolds-averaged Navier-Stokes equations. Complete solutions to the Navier-Stokes equations for fluid dynamics will require supercomputers far more powerful than those that now exist.

Though fluid dynamics has limitations, even with the computational power of today's supercomputers, the study of aerodynamics using supercomputers has shortened development time and helped designers to better predict an aircraft's design performance. To quote W. F. Ballhaus, Jr., of NASA's Ames Research Center, "Computational simulations are especially useful for the following applications:

1. making detailed fluid physics studies, such as simulations designed to shed light on the basic structure of turbulent flows;
2. developing new design concepts, such as swept forward wings or jet flaps for lift augmentation;
3. sorting through many candidate configurations and eliminating all but the most promising before wind-tunnel testing;
4. assisting the aerodynamicist in instrumenting test models to improve resolution of the physical phenomena of interest; and
5. correcting wind-tunnel data for scaling and interference errors [The use of smaller scale models, walls, and supports within the wind tunnels makes these corrections necessary]."

Describing the airflow through a jet engine is another example of a complex problem of fluid dynamics. Within a jet engine the

∇

temperatures are hot and the margins for tolerances are exceedingly small. Much like a turbine used to generate electricity, a jet engine has rows of blades that guide airflow through rotating blades within the engine. Air is compressed by the blades within the engine before thrusting from the back to push the airplane forward.

Before World War II, improvements in the efficiency of aircraft engines were achieved by trial-and-error testing and analysis of the results. More recently, designs have been tested using numerical simulations of simplified models. For example, the effects of drag due to the viscosity of the air may be analyzed separately from the flow of the air through a single row of the engine's turbine blades.

Jet engines have been improved by use of large fans placed within the engine to drive incoming air around the turbine. An unducted fan, which is like a multiblade propeller or a set of counter-rotating propellers, also improves jet engine performance. Unducted fans add to a jet engine's fuel efficiency, but a disadvantage to their use is that they create more noise than other fan-jet engines.

There are other ways in which supercomputers have improved aircraft performance. Before computers were used to help design aircraft, the wing of the Boeing 747 had four parts that were used to increase lift during takeoff and landing. These included a slat on the leading edge of the wing and three wing flaps. These parts add a great deal of weight to the aircraft and are not needed during much of the flight. Engineers at Boeing used aerodynamics simulation to learn that the wing of the 747 could be redesigned using only three of the four parts and still achieve enough lift for safe takeoff and landing.

Faster supercomputers have refined the ability to show details of the flow of air over aircraft wings. For example, during a turn, an aircraft is tilted into its direction of travel at an angle called the angle of attack. When the angle of attack is moderate to high, the air flowing over the leading edge of the wing forms two spiral vortices above the wing's upper surface. The vortices create low pressure on the upper wing surface that gives the airplane additional lift. However, when the angle of attack is large, the vortices disintegrate into chaotic swirls known as vortex breakdown and the aircraft experiences a sudden loss of lift.

Research on vortex breakdown is an example of how increasing computational power in supercomputers has been applied to a nagging problem of aerodynamics. In 1978, a simulation was attempted on a CDC 7600 computer. It could solve the equations at 36,000 grid points, but failed to depict the breakdown. In 1984, a CRAY X-MP with 120,000 grid points still could not display the breakdown. Only in 1986, using a CRAY-2 capable of analyzing 800,000 grid points, could the vortex breakdown be shown.

Boeing engineers used supercomputers to revolutionize the design process for jet aircraft. With the computational power of supercomputers, details of the flow patterns of air over the wings and body of an airplane can be examined as never before possible. In addition, the complicated data can be displayed on a screen as a three-dimensional graphic that can be viewed from any angle.

An example of how supercomputer power has been used is the redesign of the way jet engines are mounted on airplane wings. Jet engines are suspended beneath the aircraft's wings on a strut called a pylon to prevent interference between the flow of air over the wing's upper surface and the flow of air through the jet engine. Two decades of wind-tunnel tests showed the presence of drag, but only with today's supercomputer computational power could the individual sources of the drag be analyzed.

On the Boeing 737, engineers found, as expected, that mounting the engine close to the wing resulted in excessive drag. The supercomputer analysis revealed the actual source of the drag, which had remained a secret for 20 years. Boeing engineers evaluated many new design ideas using the computer, and by using their findings, they were able to model a new shape for the casing around the engine. The new design allowed them to mount the engine directly onto the wing of the aircraft without causing airflow interference on the wings or in the jet engines that would reduce the airplane's performance.

In the spring of 1994, Boeing rolled out its newest, most advanced airliner, the wide-bodied 777-200. It is the world's largest twin-jet airplane and the first Boeing aircraft to be designed entirely with computers. The customers for the jet were asked what they wanted in an airplane. The airlines made suggestions that resulted in more than 1,000 design changes to make the 777 less expensive to build, operate, and service, as well as more appealing to passengers.

W. F. Ballhaus, Jr., has cited several aircraft—the C-141, the C-5A, the F-111, and additional civilian airplanes—that could have been better designed with the aid of supercomputers. Problems with these and other aircraft were often detected only at the test-flight stage of building these airplanes. Included were things like incorrect airflow over the wings or unexpected drag on the surfaces of the aircraft at velocities at or near the speed of sound. In each case, these problems resulted in expensive redesign work, delays in production, less-efficient performance, and fewer years that the airplanes were in service.

Scientists at NASA's Ames Research Center used supercomputer simulation to examine a problem in the design of the engine for the space shuttle. Ducts used to carry hydrogen fuel into the combustion chamber of the engine had several locations where they bent at a severe angle. The supercomputer simulation displayed the areas where the flow of fuel was being held back, reducing the power of the thrust from the engine. The angles of the ducts that constrained fuel flow were redesigned using the supercomputer's simulation to produce optimum results in performance.

The Boeing 777 wide-bodied advanced airliner is the first Boeing aircraft to be designed entirely with computers. (Courtesy Boeing Commercial Airplane Group)

In another study done by scientists at NASA's Ames Research Center, supercomputers were used to simulate the flow of air past the space shuttle during its launch into orbit. Graphic representation of the areas of pressure on the space shuttle riding piggyback on its rocket ride toward space can be shown in a full-color supercomputer simulation. Engineers see the areas of highest pressure as white areas and the areas of lowest pressure as blue areas, for example. Other colors indicate intermediate levels of pressure. In one simulation, the right half of the image pictures actual pressures that were measured by sensors while the left half of the image pictures the pressures predicted by a supercomputer.

Plans for a hypersonic space plane that could thrust itself into orbit as well as take off and land like a conventional airplane instead of vertically like a rocket have been designed by NASA scientists and private industry. If this new vehicle is built, it will be more efficient and economical than the space shuttle to transport supplies as well as people into orbit. Researchers at Rockwell International who have worked on the design for the hypersonic space plane say it would be impossible to consider such a concept without the power of supercomputer computation and simulation.

The rocket now used to propel the space shuttle into orbit needs to carry with it oxygen-rich chemicals in order to properly

A computer simulation showing surface-particle paths over the space shuttle orbiter using an IRIS graphics workstation. (Courtesy NASA)

burn its fuel supply to reach orbit. The hypersonic space plane could be outfitted with a supersonic combustion RAM jet, sometimes called a scramjet, that would be able to utilize oxygen in the atmosphere, even at high altitudes where it is scarce. The airflow through the scramjet is supersonic (faster than the speed of sound). Using hydrogen fuel, the space plane will be able to reach altitudes as high as 200,000 feet and to fly at speeds as high as Mach 25. (The Mach number compares the speed of a plane to the speed of sound in the air.)

Scientists have used supercomputer models of the space plane to determine the flow of air over the body of the plane and through the scramjet engine. They have sought the best designs for the space plane's fuselage and engine by trying a succession of supercomputer simulations. Even the behavior of molecules of nitrogen and oxygen in the air would be affected by the shock of the space plane passing through the atmosphere. Thomas Edwards and Jolen Flores at Ames Research Center have studied several chemical reactions that would occur as air streams by the body of the space plane. The further study of these reactions requires teraflop supercomputers.

Supercomputers Are Designing Better Automobiles and Backhoe Loaders

More down to Earth is the use of supercomputers to design and build automobiles. Today, all parts of an automobile can be simulated by a supercomputer. Everything from airflow, noise, vibrations, and stresses around, in, or on automobile structure can be researched with a supercomputer. One area of great importance to automobile manufacturers and to the environment is the improvement of performance and efficiency of the internal combustion engine to save fuel.

Two ways to increase fuel efficiency are to reduce the aerodynamic drag caused by the flow of air over the automobile's body as it travels and to improve the combustion of gasoline in the engine.

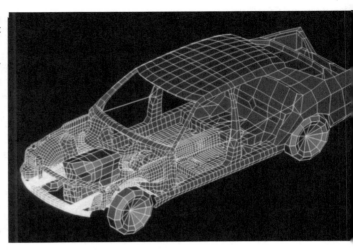

The image shows a computer simulation of a Mercedes automobile. (Courtesy Cray Research, Inc.)

Studying the complex events that happen within an automobile engine includes modeling the flow of fuel and air through ports and valves in the intake system and in the combustion chamber of each piston of the engine. The supercomputer must incorporate data about temperature and compression as well. Simulating ignition and combustion in the engine's cylinders uses the full capabilities of the supercomputer, and after combustion, the supercomputer must simulate the chemical reactions that occur when the fuel burns.

Supercomputer simulations have helped designers increase fuel economy by showing which body shapes produce the least drag as they travel through the air. Kunio Kuwahara of the Institute of Computational Fluid Dynamics in Tokyo and his colleague Susumu Shirayama have done difficult aerodynamic simulations of automobiles, which include the flow of air around the tires. They have shown how the flow of air around the tires results in turbulence at the back of the automobile, but also that the airflow over the upper body of the car is largely unaffected by this turbulence.

Another company that is using supercomputers to help design its products is Caterpillar Inc. of Peoria, Illinois—maker of track-type tractors, backhoe loaders, and other heavy equipment. The machinery is used to dig foundations for buildings, load trucks, and haul loose materials such as crushed stone, as well as in large construction projects such as road building. On April 19, 1993 Caterpillar Inc. received the National Center for Supercomputing Applications' top corporate honor in recognition for its use of high-performance computing and simulation using virtual reality to design its machines.

One of the goals of the design work is to improve visibility for the drivers in the cabs of the Caterpillar machines. Good visibility is essential for the driver's productivity and safety. Using the power of supercomputers and blueprints of the work, Caterpillar's engineers Dave Stevenson and John Bettner simulated three-dimensional working models. The engineers could see how their designs would work as the supercomputer analyzed hundreds of thousands of computations to simulate the operation of the machine.

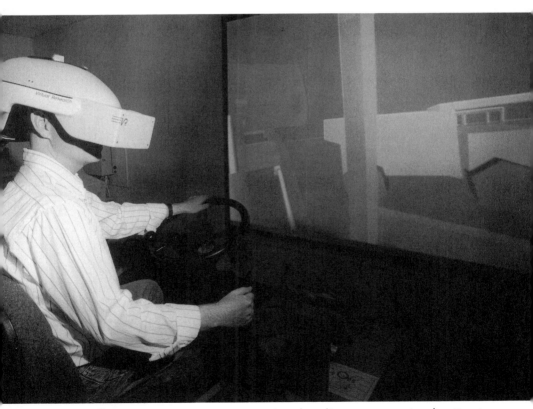

A Caterpillar Inc. test engineer using a virtual reality computer visualization to simulate operating a backhoe loader. (Courtesy Caterpillar Inc.)

"This technology allows us to shorten dramatically the amount of time it takes to analyze a new design concept and incorporate it into our production process," says Caterpillar engineer Dave Stevenson. "It also represents a sizable cost savings because we aren't having to build prototype machines or make last-minute design changes." In the past, Stevenson says that six to nine months were spent constructing full-scale models of machines, evaluating their design, and then making changes. With supercomputer simulation using virtual reality, many designs can be analyzed in less than a month.

Another idea that Caterpillar has in mind is to let its customers "field test" new designs of their machines using computer simulation and virtual reality. Meanwhile, Caterpillar engineers are receiving training and experience with the latest ways to use supercomputers to assist in the design of their machinery. Many unique technological features have resulted from the supercomputer design research that make Caterpillar's machines more reliable, powerful, and safe. Caterpillar formed a partnership with NCSA in August 1989 that helps the company remain globally competitive and a leader in the manufacture of its earth-moving and construction products.

11
∇

SUPERCOMPUTERS AND VIRTUAL REALITY

*S*upercomputers are used to create virtual reality (VR). Virtual reality is the simulation of a three-dimensional environment that appears real to the viewer. A virtual reality simulation happens in real time or as the viewer watches. The viewer can manipulate the surroundings that he or she sees during a virtual reality simulation. Though virtual reality is considered to be an industry still in its infancy, the applications for virtual reality seem limited only by our imaginations. The term *virtual reality* is credited to Jaron Lanier who founded a company named VPL Research.

Virtual reality evolved from flight and visual simulations and from attempts to assist human interaction with computers. The virtual reality experience needs to be credible, especially when its purpose is to enhance human creativity and productivity. To be perceived by the viewer as "real," the environment created in virtual reality must react appropriately to the actions of the human participant. For this reason, VR must focus the viewer's attention and thus enable the viewer to suspend disbelief about how the environment is created.

Virtual reality provides new and helpful ways for people to interact with computers, machines, and other people. For example, in areas such as education and medicine, simulation using virtual reality can provide realistic experiences, such as practicing specific surgical techniques before attempting an actual operation. Additional uses for the technology of virtual reality are as diverse as training in procedures, remote exploration of planetary surfaces, visual analysis of data, scientific visualization, and entertainment. Scientists exploring human behaviors also seek to use virtual reality to investigate the human factors that affect the interactions between people and between people and machines. In turn, this research may lead to improved ways to create virtual reality environments.

How Do Virtual Reality Environments Work?

Three types of hardware are used to create a virtual reality environment. Sensors are used to detect the viewer's reactions or move-

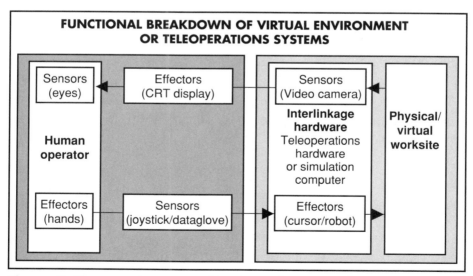

Figure 7 There are three types of hardware that are used to create a virtual environment: sensors; effectors; and special hardware, such as a supercomputer, that links the sensors and effectors to produce a realistic sensory environment.

∇

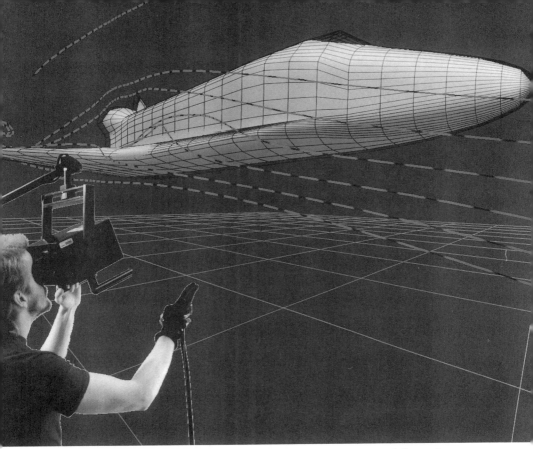

The NASA Ames Virtual Windtunnel is used for the analysis of three-dimensional computer-simulated flows of particles over the space shuttle. A glove controller is used for placing tracer particles within the flow. The user actually sees the image inside the virtual windtunnel. (Courtesy NASA)

ments, effectors are used to stimulate the viewer's senses, and special hardware links the sensors and effectors to create the illusion of a "real" physical environment. In virtual reality, the hardware that links the sensors and the effectors is a supercomputer.

For many virtual reality environments, the viewer wears a head-mounted display that uses robot manipulators, various control systems, and cameras located at a remote site to achieve the realistic VR effect. When the simulation is interactive, the viewer feels immersed directly into the VR environment. The hardware that produces the illusion usually is worn rather than entered, as it is in a traditional flight simulation.

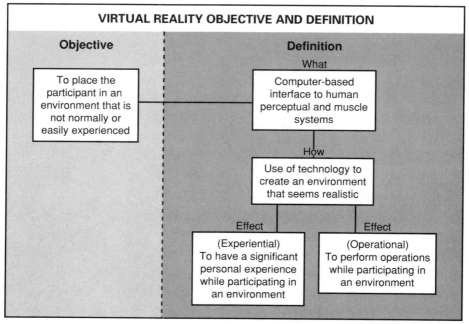

Figure 8 This chart shows the objective and definition of a virtual reality environment.

Origins of Virtual Reality

Much of the technology for virtual reality has developed from early attempts to simulate flight. In the late 1920s, Edwin Link did work in vehicle simulation, and one of the first head-mounted displays was the CAE fiber-optic helmet-mounted display, which was designed to replace larger, more expensive dome-projection flight simulators. Argonne National Laboratory and Philco both did work on simulation displays using head-mounted, closed-circuit television systems. Ivan Sutherland is one of the pioneers in personalized graphics simulation and created the first synthetic computer-generated display used for virtual environments.

The National Aeronautical and Space Administration has many applications for virtual reality simulations and has pursued development of scientific visualization, computer graphics, and the use of robotics to do remote tasks. For example, NASA has used a robot named Dante II to enter and explore the inside of Mount

Spurr, an active volcano in Alaska, an environment that is too dangerous for a human to enter.

Virtual Reality Gear

NASA uses virtual reality to develop techniques for programming robots in a simulated remote-task environment. The worker uses a special dataglove to control pop-up menus and computer graphics as he or she interacts with the robot. A series of head-mounted

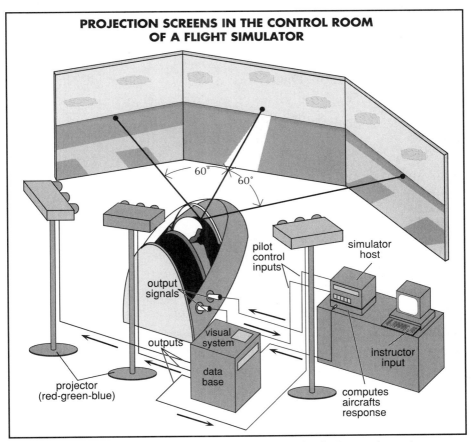

Figure 9 This diagram shows the control room of a flight simulator that uses projection screens to simulate the flight path seen by a pilot.

displays have been developed since 1985 by NASA at the Ames Research Center to test performance.

The U.S. military also is developing virtual reality flight simulators. Both the U.S. Airforce and the U.S. Navy have been working on systems to use in training of crews, to provide real-time mission updates, and to control operations and enforcement of the military rules of engagement. With the visually coupled airborne simulator (VCASS), a pilot is immersed in a fully-simulated environment and can "fly" the airplane under combat conditions using hand gestures, head and eye movements, and voice commands. The VCASS-based system is also being used to develop an integrated control of future combat aircraft known as microcomputer application of graphics with interactive communications (MAGIC).

Recently, less expensive virtual reality environment systems have become available to the public. They include Fakespace BOOM and n-Vision Datavisor, as well as helmet displays from Sega and Sony. Generally, the virtual reality environments created by these systems are not as demanding as those needed for use in simulation of actual flight, either commercially or for the military.

In the search for better ways to interact with computers and their applications, gloves have become important devices. People perform most of their everyday tasks using their hands, so they seem like a very natural way to interact with the surrounding environment, including machines and computers. When interacting with computers, people use joy sticks, keyboards, and mice, but these devices tend to be clumsy and do not allow us to use the extraordinary dexterity of our hands to best advantage.

Electronic gloves have been designed as a way to utilize the natural dexterity of human hands to interact with computers. The concept allows the hand to be used as a tool to point, select, reach, and even grab information or objects seen on a computer screen or in a virtual reality environment.

In the 1970s researchers at the MIT Architecture Machine Group demonstrated how hand motion could be interpreted and used as input information to computers. In a project called "Put-that-there," a sensor called Polhemus 3 was used to track and

The equipment for the Virtual Interactive Environment Workstation (VIEW) creates a three-dimensional display system which allows users to experience remote environments such as the space station or the surface of Mars without actually being there. (Courtesy NASA)

communicate the position of the user's hand to the computer. With this device, the user could point exactly to a specific point on a large wall display, and using this information, the person could select items of interest, move them from one location to another on the display screen, and ask questions about the item.

From these beginnings, electronic gloves have been developed that use position tracking to determine the position of the hand and various glove technologies to determine the shape of the hand. Locating the position of the hand in three-dimensional space uses technologies such as cameras that watch the hand from a distance, a magnetic field such as that used by the Polhemus device, or ultrasonic "pings" to locate the hand acoustically.

Several efforts have been made to measure the shape of the hand as the palm and fingers flex. One example is the MIT LED glove. In the early 1980s scientists at the MIT Architecture Machine Group and at the MIT Media Lab built a device using a camera-based LED system that could track limb and body positions for computer graphics animation. The glove included in this work used devices known as light emitting diodes, or LEDs, to track the motion of the hand.

Additional gloves with various devices and sensors in them were designed by other researchers. Gary Grimes of Bell Telephone Laboratories developed a cloth glove that could recognize the Single Hand Manual Alphabet for the American Deaf (1983). Thomas Zimmerman and others worked on the VPL DataGlove (1987). It is made of Lycra and has optical fibers along the backs of the fingers. When a finger is bent, the brightness of the light passing through the optical fibers changes and the change is transmitted to a processor that determines the position of the finger. The DataGlove was reasonably priced, so it has seen widespread use all over the world.

The Mattel toy company manufactured an inexpensive glove in 1989 to use to control home video games like Nintendo. The glove is vinyl with a Lycra palm. Sensors built into the backs of the fingers of the glove keep track of the position of the fingers. Acoustic trackers located on the back of the hand locate the position of the glove in relation to another tracker on the television monitor for the video game. The glove works with several video games and can be used to control motions such as the swinging punch of a boxer on the television screen. Commercially, the VPL DataGlove and the Mattel Power Glove gave a strong push to the development of electronic gloves as an interface with computers and computer-controlled devices.

James Kramer of Stanford University developed the Cyber-Glove in an effort to translate the motions of American sign language into spoken English. This is a cloth glove with up to 22 thin foil strain gauges sewn into it to detect finger and wrist motions and flexing. As with some of the other gloves, a tracker is mounted on the glove to locate the hand's position and signals from the glove are converted into a stream of digital data that can be read by a computer. The performance of the CyberGlove is accurate, relatively smooth, and well suited for doing fine manipulations.

The MIT Media Lab has demonstrated the operation of a simulated construction crane using hand signals that are conventional at construction sites. The same system has been used to control point of view, locomotion, selections, and manipulations for the teleoperation of a six-legged robot.

Supercomputers and Animation for Entertainment

Animation of characters in films now often uses a key-frame technique that is not much different than traditional hand animation in which artists drew and colored all the frames. Computers create additional frames to fill in the action between key frames done by artists and to give a smooth quality to the motion of the characters. Depending on how smooth the transition is from one frame to the next, the quality may be quite mechanical, subtly unnatural, or almost lifelike.

Some animation companies have started to use puppets and body tracking to capture motion that can later be interpreted by computer into animated characters. In this way, the fine nuances of natural motion can be transferred to computer-created characters. The process creates animated characters that seem very lifelike.

In 1989 Jim Henson and Pacific Data Images worked together to produce a computer-generated character whose body movements could follow those of conventional puppets. They built a one-handed device that allowed the puppeteer to control the motion of the character on the computer graphics screen as well as the character's mouth movements.

Another animator at Videosystem in France, Geoff Levner, used DataGloves, joysticks, foot pedals, and other devices to develop a real-time computer animation system called PORC (Puppets Orchestrated in Real-time by Computer). As an example, Poupidoo, a computer puppet, anchored a 24-hour-long animation marathon on French television.

Poupidoo was controlled by three puppeteers. One used a glove to control the expression and shape of the computer puppet's mouth, while the second used a glove to control the expression and closing of the eyes and a joystick to choose the direction of the puppet's glance. The third puppeteer used two gloves as well as a

Lifelike animation of a cartoon character's face is accomplished in real time using special computer software with a camera system that is tracking the expressions on a human actor's face. (Courtesy Adaptive Optics Associates, Inc.)

A two camera Multi-Trax system for capturing motion in three dimensions. Up to seven cameras may be used in a Multi–Trax system. (Courtesy Adaptive Optics Associates, Inc.)

set of Polhemus trackers to control Poupidoo's arms and upper-body motions.

GreyStone Technology Inc. is a manufacturer of simulation software for military use. However, the company also is producing software applications for entertainment. In 1993 they demonstrated their first application, a real-time virtual reality experience called the Pteranodon. The participant goes for a ride on the back of a mythical prehistoric Pteranodon in which he or she can fly down a narrow canyon alive with giant insects and flying bats, descend under rocky arches, and whoosh over waterfalls. The rider can circle Castle GreyStone in which a fierce dragon lives.

Since introducing the Pteranodon, GreyStone Technology, Inc. has added Chameleon 500 and Thunderbolt and Labyrinth Rangers for the Chameleon Corporation, as well as other virtual reality experiences. For example, with the Chameleon VR, a centrifugelike gondola with two to ten arms is used to seat two people. As the gondola rotates, the riders experience gravitational, or G, forces that coincide with what they are experiencing from the VR program. The Chameleon 500 is a VR racing experience that is similar to the Indianapolis 500. Other cars are driven by the computer and the driver pits his or her skills against them.

At the MIT Media Lab, Tod Machover used an Exos DHM (Dexterous HandMaster) glove to control the acoustics in live musical performances. In a musical piece titled "bug-mundra," two guitarists and a percussionist provide input to a computer-music system that reshapes sounds and synthesizes new ones. During the performance, the conductor, wearing a DHM on the left hand, controls the timbre and volume of various sounds. The piece "bug-mundra" had its premier in Tokyo in 1990 and has also been performed in various places in the United States and Europe.

In another computer music system that follows a human conductor, Jideyki Morita uses a glove to conduct a synthetic orchestra. The conductor has an infrared light on the end of the baton held in the right hand and a DataGlove and tracker on the left hand. A special camera follows the baton, the tracker, and the DataGlove. Information from the left hand is interpreted to determine musical expressions such as vibrato, crescendo, and dolce. The resulting synthetic music system interprets the conductor's conventional way of communicating with more finely tuned expression.

Virtual reality has many practical applications. For instance, VR can be used as a design tool for architecture. One challenge is to create multiuser VR systems that allow for input from two or more people. Perhaps a couple wish to design a house together, for example.

To get started, one partner may choose the front wall of the house with a doorway cut into it. Next, the user can properly position the wall of the house. Meanwhile, the other partner suggests some adjustments to the wall. By pressing a joy stick, the user can see several types of outside finishes to select for the front wall of the house, such as bricks, granite, or wood clapboards.

While this is going on, the second partner chooses from among several options for the slope of the roof, its orientation to the front

∇

wall, and the roofing material to cover it. Selections continue until the outside of the house is complete.

Next, one partner uses a wand to change the perspective. Now, the couple find themselves able to enter and wander through the interior of the house, getting a sense of how it will feel to walk through its doorways and look out through its windows. After returning outside again, the couple can add landscaping to complete the building of their virtual reality house.

The Workroom is a system developed by Sense8 and the Institute for Simulation and Training at the University of Central Florida representing an application of a collaborative design system using VR technologies. Its virtual reality house-building system demonstrates the ease with which virtual environments can assist with difficult design tasks.

Multiple user virtual reality environments provide people with new ways to interact with each other. In addition, multiple-user virtual reality offers new ways to jointly work on design problems, interact with remote sites, and explore new situations before the actual experience.

CONCLUSION

The computational power of supercomputers has taken dramatic strides forward in recent years, and the explosive pace of growth will continue into the age of teraflops and beyond. Supercomputers, linked together through dedicated computer networks, have produced a new information reality with rapidly expanding vistas in all fields of learning and research.

Supercomputers are providing researchers all over the world with access to more data and better ways to explore, analyze, manipulate, visualize, and interact with that data. More and more, researchers are consulting with each other and working together toward solving complex problems of mutual interest. Scientists are studying weather patterns worldwide and creating climate models in an effort to better understand and predict weather. Supercomputers have enabled researchers to recreate models of ancient climates as a way to verify the accuracy of their predictive models.

The control of agricultural pests is being studied using supercomputers. The evaluation of biological control methods, combined with integrated pest-management methods, may allow farmers to significantly reduce the use of pesticides and still obtain reasonable crop yields.

The Human Genome Project has progressed much faster than scientists anticipated, and supercomputers are needed to catalog data and make it accessible to other researchers. Many of the findings about human genes may lead the way to new treatments for genetically caused diseases.

Supercomputers are being used to study black holes and gravitational waves, how galaxies were formed, and many intriguing questions about the origin of the universe itself. New materials are being created using visualization techniques made possible by the computational power of supercomputers. Scientists have been able to decipher the fundamental particles that make up all matter in the universe—in essence, what everything is made of—with the help of supercomputers.

In industry, supercomputers are used to design better automobiles, airplanes, and space vehicles. Research on the dynamics of

Grade school students are shown working with a technician using MacIntosh computers in the machine room at NCSA. (Courtesy National Center for Supercomputing Applications)

airflow over airplane fuselage and wing surfaces, for example, has improved the design and efficiency of new aircraft. With the advent of virtual reality environments, scientists can simulate and experience remote or hostile locations, such as the surface of Mars. In the field of entertainment, lifelike animation is being achieved using supercomputers.

Supercomputers are shaping the future by advancing the store of human knowledge that we have available to us in accessible data banks. By transforming and enhancing the way we learn, and by helping us to find answers to the grand-challenge problems, supercomputers have the power to enrich our understanding of ourselves and of the very nature of the universe.

GLOSSARY

Terms in the glossary appear in *italics* the first time they are used in the text.

absolute zero   The temperature at which the molecules in matter stop moving and contain no heat or energy. Absolute zero is equivalent to −273.15 degrees Celsius (− 459.67 degrees Fahrenheit), or 273.15 degrees below the freezing point of water.

amino acid   There are 20 amino acids that are the basic building blocks of all of the proteins found in living organisms. *See also* gene and nucleotide.

antimatter   Matter that consists of atoms with negatively charged nuclei and positively charged electrons. Antimatter is the opposite of the matter that we observe in the universe, which has positively charged nuclei and negatively charged electrons.

applications program   The set of instructions that direct a computer to perform the specific tasks necessary to solve a problem or to analyze or store data.

architecture   The design of a computer system that controls how the computer processes data. For example, a computer with the von Neumann architecture has one central processor in which each operation is performed serially, in a sequence of single steps.

binary number system   A system in which numbers and letters are represented by only two digits, 0 and 1. Our commonly used decimal number system uses the 10 digits 0 through 9.

The binary number system is well suited to computers because an electrical switch that is OFF can represent zero and an electrical switch that is ON can represent 1.

black hole   A black hole is believed to be a star that has collapsed into a dense mass with a gravitational force so powerful that even light cannot escape.

boson   The group of subatomic particles that is represented by the basic unit of light called the photon. Bosons control interactions between matter and carry the four basic forces of nature: gravity, electromagnetism, and what physicists call the "weak" and "strong" forces. *See* fermion.

central processing unit (CPU)   The central part or "brains" of the computer that actually carries out calculations and acts upon instructions.

coarse-grained system   A computer system that uses only a few full-scale processors.

compiler   A computer program that translates the instruction in a symbolic language such as FORTRAN into machine language that the computer can understand and use.

conductor   A material, such as the metal copper, which allows electricity to flow through it easily.

daemon   The process that continuously runs in the background of a hypercomputer and that consists of a scheduler and an allocator, which distribute the tasks to be performed by the processors within the hypercomputer network. *See* hypercomputer.

data parallelism   A technique in which the computer simultaneously does the same operation on many portions of the data needed to solve a problem. This method allows the rate of processing to be increased by factors that are determined by the amount of data to be processed, not by the number of steps in an operation.

debugging   The process of eliminating errors or malfunctions that are preventing a computer or computer program from operating correctly.

▽

deoxyribonucleic acid (DNA) The genetic material found in living organisms. DNA molecules consist of long sequences of smaller units called nucleotides. DNA molecules contain coded information (genes) that determines the characteristics of each living organism. *See also* nucleotide.

fermion The group of subatomic particles that consists of electrons, protons, and neutrons. *See* boson.

fifth-generation computers Computers of this generation use ultra-large-scale integration (ULSI; from 2 to 64 million transistors on a chip) and reflect new design architectures as well as new logic-based languages.

fine-grained system A computer system that uses large numbers of less-powerful processors.

first-generation computers (1951–58) Computers characterized by vacuum tubes, magnetic drums for memory, and punched cards for input and output, as well as external storage.

flops This term stands for "floating point operations per second." It is a measure of the speed of performance of a computer.

fluid dynamics The branch of physics that studies the complex flow of gases and liquids.

fourth-generation computers (1971–) Computers characterized by large-scale integrated (LSI) circuits and more currently with very large-scale integrated circuits (VLSI) that may consist of millions of transistors. These computers have enough memory capacity to allow the processing of enormous quantities of data and thousands of simultaneous users. Input and output can be from a variety of sources such as keyboards, printers, optical scanners, and touch screens.

functional parallelism A method of parallel processing in which the computer operates simultaneously on separate parts of the data needed to solve a problem. Each operation is kept separate until the resultant data can be combined to reach an answer.

gene A gene is a sequence of nucleotide bases on the DNA molecule that determines the order of amino acids in a protein molecule. Genes determine the characteristics of living organisms.

gluon   Particles that carry what physicists call the strong force, or the attraction that binds quarks together. *See* quark.

hyperchannel   The main carrier of information in a supercomputer that links all of the parts.

hypercomputer   A parallel computer system that consists of the idle processors in a network of personal computers. For example, a company may have a network of workstation personal computers in which the processors in its computers are idle as much as half of the time. If the company can access the free time of each of the processors in its network, it effectively owns a multiprocessor parallel computer.

input/output (I/O)   Input is the data or information that the user enters into the computer, and output is the result of running a problem or set of calculations through the computer. Supercomputers have extremely high rates of I/O processing.

insulator   A material that does not allow electricity to pass through it, such as glass, rubber, or plastic.

integrated circuit (IC)   A complete electric circuit consisting of transistors and other components, manufactured on a single silicon chip. Large scale integration (LSI) and very large scale integration (VLSI) are terms that indicate thousands or tens of thousands of transistors and other components on a single silicon chip.

lepton   A type of basic building block of matter. There are three pairs of leptons, but these are far less massive than quarks. *See* quark.

memory   Stored instructions and data in a computer that can be accessed during computations. In a multiprocessor computer, each processor may have its own memory, may share a central memory, or may have a combination of both.

microprocessor   A computer chip that has all of the components of the central processing unit (CPU) of a computer. Also called a "computer on a chip."

modem   A device that transforms digital data from a computer into analog form, which can be transmitted over communication lines such as telephone lines. The word *modem* is from the terms *mo*dulation-*dem*odulation, which describe the process. A modem can also receive data in an analog form and restore it to digital form so that information can flow both to and from a computer.

nanosecond   One billionth of a second.

node   An individual processor that is part of a computer processing network.

nucleotide   The unit of structure of the DNA or RNA molecule. Each nucleotide consists of a molecule of sugar, a phosphate group, and a base. DNA has four bases known as adenine (A), guanine (G), thymine (T), and cytosine (C). A sequence of three nucleotide bases along the DNA molecule contains the code for one amino acid. Amino acids are the building blocks of protein molecules. *See* deoxyribonucleic acid.

operating clock speed   The smallest interval of time in which synchronized operations take place within a computer.

operating program or system   The set of instructions that oversees the workings of the computer itself.

parallel processing   The execution of several operations or several parts of an operation on a computer at the same time. Typically the term applies to computers that have more than one processor or even a very large number of processors.

perovskite   A kind of ceramic material with a crystalline structure that behaves somewhat like a metal. Some perovskites are superconductors at relatively high temperatures.

pipelining   One method of parallel processing in which several computer operations may occur at the same time, such as readying data, calculating sums, and storing results of previous operations.

pixel   The smallest unit of a display of an electronically coded picture image. The word is derived from the term *picture element*. For example, a color picture seen on a computer screen is made up of many small individual units of color, or pixels, that together form the image.

program The instructions that direct a computer to perform the tasks necessary to solve a problem, analyze data, or store information.

protocol A standard format that controls the communications within a computer.

quark The smaller particles that make up protons and neutrons. There are three pairs of quarks, which are basic building blocks of matter. Unlike other subatomic particles, quarks have fractional charges. Quarks are named after a nonsense syllable that Murray Gell-Mann read in a passage from James Joyce's *Finnegan's Wake*.

quark confinement The behavior exhibited as a quark moves away from the other two quarks present within a proton or neutron; when this happens, the other two quarks pull on it with a force so strong that the proton or neutron is kept whole.

real time The actual time in which a process or event takes place. For example, within a virtual reality environment, a process or event appears to the viewer to be happening as he or she watches or participates.

second-generation computers (1959–64) Computers characterized by transistors (which replaced vacuum tubes), magnetic cores for memory, and magnetic tape for input and output as well as external storage of data.

semiconductor A substance that is neither a good insulator nor a good conductor of electricity. Its properties can be altered with doping materials so that it can serve as either an insulator or a conductor. Silicon, which is found in ordinary sand, is commonly used as a semiconductor material.

supercomputer The fastest, most powerful computers available in the world. Supercomputers can do large-scale scientific calculations and can rapidly analyze enormous quantities of data.

superconductor A material that can conduct electricity with no resistance.

third-generation computers (1964–70) Computers characterized by integrated circuits (which replaced transistors). Magnetic tape, magnetic disks, and packs of disks were used for storage of data. The operating systems of these computers allowed for multiple, simultaneous use. Third-generation computers could process as many as 10 million instructions per second.

transistor A solid-state electronic device that is much smaller and that generates far less heat than a vacuum tube. These characteristics of transistors allowed computers to be built that were much lighter and more compact in size. Hence, transistors quickly replaced the switching function of vacuum tubes in computers.

tuple space A kind of shared memory in which the items in the memory have no computer address. In effect, this means that any task in tuple space can be accessed without regard to its physical location or the order of the items to be processed.

vacuum tube An electron tube that looks like an elongated lightbulb with a metal filament inside and that has had the air inside it removed. Vacuum tubes were used as switches in early computers such as ENIAC.

vector processing Calculations performed on a computer in which a single instruction, such as adding or multiplying, is carried out simultaneously on an entire list of numbers. Vector processing speeds up the calculation of answers.

virtual reality (VR) Virtual reality is the simulation of a three-dimensional environment that appears real to the viewer.

FURTHER READING

Billings, Charlene W. *Microchip: Small Wonder*. New York: Dodd, Mead/Putnam's, 1984. This 48-page book introduces microchips, the binary system, and describes how microchips work.
————. *Superconductivity: From Discovery to Breakthrough*. New York: Cobblehill Books/Dutton, 1991. This 64-page book introduces the phenomenon of superconductivity; how it was discovered, its importance, and how it currently is being used. The race to find high-temperature superconductors is described.
Carter, Alden R. and LeBlanc, Wayne J. *Supercomputers*. New York: Franklin Watts, 1985. An introduction to supercomputers that includes explanations of supercomputer processing techniques, uses of supercomputers, and a glossary.
Karin, Sidney and Smith, Norris P. *The Supercomputer Era*. New York: Harcourt Brace Jovanovich, 1987. An adult-length book describing the age of supercomputers and how supercomputers are being used in science and industry.
Kaufmann, William J., III and Smarr, Larry L. *Supercomputing and the Transformation of Science*. New York: Scientific American Library, 1993. An adult-length book describing supercomputers and illustrated with abundant color photographs and drawings.
Metropolis, N. and Rota, Gian-Carlo, editors. *A New Era in Computation*. Cambridge, Massachusetts: MIT Press, 1993; 1992, the American Academy of Arts and Sciences. Eleven of the

articles in this volume originally appeared in the Winter 1992 issue of *Daedalus*, vol. 121, no. 1. This book includes the articles reprinted from *Daedalus* as well as additional articles that discuss the impact of massively parallel computing and super-computers on our future.

Nardo, Don. *Computers: Mechanical Minds*. San Diego, California: Lucent Books, 1990. This children's book is an introduction to computers that includes the history of their development.

Ritchie, David. *The Computer Pioneers: The Making of the Modern Computer*. New York: Simon and Schuster, 1986. This book describes the history of the development of the computer from the abacus to modern computers. It has many interesting accounts about the people who pioneered computers.

Scientific American Special Issue, Vol. 1. *Trends in Computing*. Published by the staff of *Scientific American*, New York, 1988. This special issue of *Scientific American* magazine is a collection of 18 articles about computing.

Slater, Robert. *Portraits in Silicon*. Cambridge, Massachusetts: MIT Press, 1987. This adult-length book describes the history of computers and the pioneering spirit of the people who developed them.

INDEX

Close, Frank, 91
coarse-grained system, 33, 120
Cohen, Daniel, 71
Collins, Dr. Francis, 69, 70
Colorado State University, 39
community climate model (CCM), 56
compiler, 36, 120
computational simulations, uses of, 94
computer chess and checkers, 28, 29
Computer Museum, 29
computer simulation, 53, *75*, 80, *81, 100*
computer-on-a-chip, 20, 22, 122
conductor, 18, 120, 124
Connection Machine, *34, 35*, 49, 64
Control Data Corporation (CDC), 24
CONVEX C3880 (C3), 49
Cooper, Leon N., and Cooper Pairs, 84
Cornell Theory Center, 4, 40
Cornell University, 36, 78
Courant Institute of Mathematical Sciences, 71, *72*
Covey, Curt, 63
Cray Research, Inc., *2*, 25, 27, 28
CRAY supercomputers, 21, 22, *24*, 25, *26*, 27–29, 33, 39, 41, 44, 48, 49, 55, 64, 76, 96
Cray, Seymour, 23, 24, 25, 26, 28
Cruft Laboratory, 14
Crutzen, Paul J., 63
Cyber 205, 39
CyberGlove, 110, 111
cytosine (C), 67, 123

D

daemon, 38, 120
data parallelism, 32, 120
DataGlove, 110, 112, 114
debugging, 15, 120
deoxyribonucleic acid (DNA), 67, *68*, 69–71, 121
Department of Defense's Transmission Control Protocol/Internet Protocol (TCP/IP), 45
digital computer, 7, 33
Digital Equipment Corporation (DEC), 45, 62
Digital Productions, 39
disk operating system (DOS), 43
Dixon, David, 62
Durfee, Benjamin M., 14

E

Eckert, J. Presper, 16
EDVAC, 33
Edwards, Thomas, 99
Einstein, Albert, 77, 78
El Niño, 56

Electronic Numerical Integrator and Calculator (ENIAC), *16*, 17, 22, 125
Engineering Research Associates (ERA), 23
Environmental Protection Agency (EPA), 61
ERA 1101, scientific computer, 23
European Center for Medium-range Weather Forecasts (ECMWF), 55
European Cern, 91
European corn borer, 65
Exos DHM (Dexterous HandMaster) glove, 114

F

Fairchild Semiconductor, 19, 20
Fakespace BOOM, 108
Fast Analysis Software Toolkit (FAST), *93*
Fermi Laboratory, 90
fermion, 88, 121
fifth-generation computer, 121
fine-grained system, 33, 121
firearms, manufacturing, 31
first-generation computer, 18
flight simulator, *107*
Floating Point Systems (FPS), 34, 36
floating-point operations (flops), 1, 27, 121
Flores, Jolen, 99
fluid dynamics, 93, 94, 121
FORTRAN, 36, 43, 120
Four-processor Cray Extended Architecture, *2*
fourth-generation computer, 20, 121
Freeman, Arthur J., 79, 81
full potential linearized plane wave (FLAPW), 80
Fuller, Buckminster, 86
functional parallelism, 32, 121

G

GA Technologies, Inc., 40
galaxies, 74, *75*, 76, 77, 117
galium arsenide, 28
gas dynamics, 76
Gelernter, David, 37
Gell-Mann, Murray, 88, 124
GenBank, 70
gene, 67, 121
General Agreement on Tariffs and Trade, 42
general circulation model, 52
Genethon, 71
Genome Data Base, 70
global climate, 55, 62, 63
gluon, *89*, 90, 122
Gore, Albert (U.S. vice president), 3
grand challenge problem, 4, 44, 69, 78, 118
gravitational wave, 77, 78, 117
greenhouse effect, *53*, 58–*60*, 61, 63

SDSCNET, 47, 49
SEARCH, 69
second-generation computer, 18, 124
Seidel, Ed, 78
semiconductor, 18, 81, 87, 124
SequoiaNet, 63
Shirayama, Susumu, 100
Shockley, William, 17
silicon, 18, 21, 28
Single Hand Manual Alphabet for the
    American Deaf, 110
Slichter, Charles, 85
Smagorinsky, J., 54
Smith, Douglas W., 69
space shuttle, 62, 97, 98, *105*
Sperry Rand, 23, 24
Sputnik, 19
Standard Model of the universe, 91
Stanford University, 110
Stevenson, David, 101, 102
Stokes, Sir George C., 93
STRETCH, 25
supercomputers, defined, 1, 124
Supercomputing Teacher Enhancement Pro-
    gram (STEP), 5
superconductors and superconductivity, 26,
    82, *83*, 85, 87, 123, 124
SuperQuest, 5, 6
Sutherland, Ivan, 106

T
tectonic plate, 59
Texas Instruments, 19
theory of general relativity, 77
Thinking Machines Inc., 33, *35*, 64, 86
third-generation computer, 20, 125
Thomas Paine Elementary School, 6
Thompson, Starley L., 57, 64
Thomson, William (Lord Kelvin), 83, *84*
thymine (T), 67, 123
Tinsley, Marion, 29
top-down theory, 75, 76, 77
tornadic storm, *53*
transistor, 17, *18*, 19, 22, 33, 124, 125
TTAPS study, 63, 64
tuple space, 38, 125

U
U.S. Census Bureau, 11, 13
ultraviolet radiation, 61
United States Navy Bureau of Ships, 15
UNIVAC 1103, 23

University Corporation for Atmospheric Re-
    search, 52
University of California, 86
University of Pennsylvania, 16
University of Arkansas, 85
University of California, 40, 62, 69, 80
University of Colorado, 63
University of Illinois, 40, 49, 64, 66, 76, 85
University of Minnesota, 23, 39
University of North Carolina, 70, 78
University of Pittsburgh, 78
University of Texas, 78
University of Wisconsin, 56
uracil (U), 67

V
vacuum tube, 15, *17*, 18, 19, 32, 124, 125
vector processing, 27, 125
very large scale integration (VLSI), 22, 33,
    121
Videosystem, 112
Virtual Interactive Environment Worksta-
    tion (VIEW), *109*
virtual reality (VR), 3, 6, *48*, 49, 103, *104*,
    106, 114, 117, 118, 125
Visualization Laboratory (VisLab), 46
Visually Coupled Airborne Simulator
    (VCASS), 108
von Neumann, John, 33, 36, 119
VPL DataGlove, 108, 110, 112, 114
VPL Research, 103

W
Warner, Dick, 66
Washington, Warren M., 58
Watson, Sr., Thomas, 14
weather forecasting, 3, 52, *53*, 54, 55, 116
Weinert , Michael, 80
Whitney, Eli, 31
Wimmer, Erich, 80
Woodstock of Physics, 85
World Computer Chess Championship, 28
Wu, Maw-Kuen, 83

Y
Yale University, 38, 70, 87
Younger Dryas, 57

Z
Zel'dovich, Yakob B., 75, 76
ZEUS-2D and 3D, 76, 77
Zimmerman, Jim, 6